Praise for The Sales Whisperer

"Our clients found Sales Whisperer™ concepts to be refreshing and beautifully simple in today's complex business climate. The book and the seminars will change your daily routine."
Sue Marvin, Area Manager, Chicago Title

"When I was growing up a commercial that was big was 'When E. F. Hutton speaks, people listen.' In my experience with Joe Panzica, when he talks about sales and sales technique, people should listen. I've been in sales for 30+ years and Joe improves my approach every time we meet."
David H. Vonk, PGA Golf Professional

"In a dynamic way, Joe quickly impressed me with his depth of knowledge about successful selling. I walked away with ideas I could immediately use to achieve my professional goals. Joe will be teaching at Lake Michigan College this fall."
Marge Zibbel, Associate Dean, Lake Michigan College

"Joe effectively coaches with easy to understand yet very effective techniques to make lasting differences in our interactions with people—you will enjoy this book!"
Rae German, President, 360 Associates Inc.

"Joseph offers insight and understanding into many ways of relating to people. His suggestions, recommendations, and words of encouragement have been beneficial in helping me design and implement a number of programs for ministry at Christ Lutheran Church. I am particularly grateful for his input and helpfulness in my doctoral work."
The Rev. Philip Quardokus, Senior Pastor, Christ Lutheran Church

I have known Joe personally for years and by reputation prior to that. His style is subtle yet profound, quiet yet his message shouts volumes. Joe is one of those guys you like the instant you meet him. Calling him a sales trainer is a disservice. He is more a "tried it ... did it" coach and mentor who projects the feeling you are the only person in the room, and his national awards for sales performance and education would fill a trophy room. The Sales Whisperer™ provides refreshing insights for everyone, whether in direct sales or simply in everyday life."

Tom Carson, Vice President, 360 Associates Inc.

"Joe has been a key resource in delivering high quality face to face product and skills training to our key customers. Not only has he delivered the training but his wealth of knowledge in the wholesale and retail businesses has enabled him to assist in creating and editing a great deal of the material. Joe is truly an expert in the training field.

"Joe's approach to training is pragmatic: Develop an integrated program using product as the background with retail sales skills as the driving force. Teach an associate how to sell first and then the product knowledge enhances their ability to meet the needs of their customer. In all aspects of training, Joe has always delivered a quality experience to his audience."

Doug Harbert, Sr. Sales Manager, Sales Education
Whirlpool Corporation

THE SALES WHISPERER

Success-Proven Techniques and Approaches to the Psychology of Selling

JOE PANZICA

WingSpan Press

Copyright © 2007 by Joe Panzica
All rights reserved.

No part of this book may be used or reproduced in any manner
without written permission of the author, except for brief quotations
used in reviews and critiques.

Printed in the United States of America

Published by WingSpan Press, Livermore, CA
www.wingspanpress.com

The WingSpan name, logo and colophon are the trademarks of
WingSpan Publishing.

ISBN 978-1-59594-193-0

First edition 2007

Library of Congress Control Number 2007935026

The Sales Whisperer is a registered trademark of Joe
Panzica, Sales Whisperer.

To my wife Mary, my daughters Stacy and Jennifer, their husbands, and my grandchildren.

A personal note to the readers of this book:

I've trained salespeople all over the United States and in Mexico and Puerto Rico. I have more than 30 years of sales experience, nearly 29 of that with Whirlpool Corporation.

I have taught workshops and symposiums on Retail Salesmanship; Coaching and Counseling Peers and Subordinates; and Add-on sales. I have benched-marked winning practices and observed the bad habits that prevent a salesperson from rising to the top.

I know salespeople. I am one.

It was at the urging of my friend Tom Carson, Vice-President of 360 Associates, Inc., as well as the sales professionals who have taken my workshops, that I wrote this book. It's my intention to share my insights and experience, to get to the point rapidly, and to make sure you have a thorough understanding of the material.

I have designed the book to be a quick and easy read. I know that salespeople have short attention spans. We want to get to the bottom line quickly. For that reason I don't spend a lot of time on theory and the research behind it, but instead deliver successful, time-tested selling principles based on human psychology and the differences in the way men and women think, how executives (male and female) think, and what consumers are hoping to hear from those of us in the selling profession.

I reveal many helpful secrets to those who are interested in excelling in all kinds of sales, both those driven by the cash rewards and promotional opportunities, and those who are driven by the notion of public acclaim and the personal satisfaction of being the best.

Each chapter stands alone so that you may use any section as a refresher, but I must stress that the Sales Whisperer™ program is an integrated system: each segment is uniquely singular but together profoundly plural. The system works if you follow it. All of it.

If you read with an open mind, I'm confident that you will learn more about the power of persuasion and human nature (and how to control it, particularly when it comes to sales) than I picked up in many weeks of formal training.

I heard a story a while back about a man who prayed for patience. He said, "Lord please grant me patience—and grant it to me NOW!" That's who we sales professionals are. That's how we learn. That's how I've written this book. Enjoy the read.

Joe Panzica
The Sales Whisperer™

Contents

Introduction

We all sell every day. Some sales are obvious, such as selling goods and services at retail or wholesale. Others are not so obvious: most people don't think about an interview or negotiating with a supplier as sales, but they are.

There is a science to selling, and the Sales Whisperer™ program brings winning, time-tested techniques into focus. Understanding the psychology of human emotions and applying these techniques will work for the homemaker, church board member, or PTA leader as well as the professional salesperson. From engineer to lawyer, doctor to machine operator, CEO to soccer mom, the principles in this book will improve your daily efficiency and your overall success.

They have been used successfully across the United States, Mexico, and even in Puerto Rico. Sales Whisperer™ techniques have also proved successful in college interviews, job interviews, and even for those interviewing for a promotion with their current employer!

Welcome to my world, the world of the Sales Whisperer™.

Chapter 1

The Principles of Persuasion

For many years, I've depended on psychology for success in sales. Based on many years of experience in sales and in the mentoring of others, the Sales Whisperer™ psychology has proven to be extremely effective in both retail and wholesale sales, particularly on big-ticket items. It has also proven successful in sales of intangible products such as life insurance, concepts, or ideas.

The Sales Whisperer™ program is an integrated system. Each element is UNIQUELY SINGULAR in that using any one of the elements is effective. It is also PROFOUNDLY PLURAL, for each element builds on the others to maximize effectiveness. Does it work 100% of the time? If it did, I'd be perfect in sales. Nothing works 100% of the time. Nobody I've ever met bats a thousand. It does work a very high percentage of the time, though, and very high percentages are what you want in Las Vegas—and in sales.

Briefly, the Sales Whisperer™ technique relies on six principles of psychology to create an environment in which the consumer places implicit trust in the sales professional's ability to guide them through the buying process. I refer to the establishment of this implicit trust as putting the consumer into a calm, submissive state. Before the consumer even walks through the door of your company or place of business, you should have a thorough understanding of them. Everything that follows depends on these principles:

Mutual Interchange
Entrusting
Image
Safety in Numbers
Follow Me
Insufficient Supply/Time

Principle #1: Mutual Interchange

The sales transaction is one of mutual interchange: the consumer has a problem that needs resolution and which he or she depends on the salesperson to fix; in exchange for resolving the consumer's problem, you, the salesperson, make money for your company. And, if you're working on commission, for yourself.

The critical element here is sincerity. If the consumer doesn't buy in to your sincerity, you lose a valuable tool for gaining early control of the selling situation. Please understand that in no way do I tolerate, appreciate, or advocate high-pressure selling. I contend—and proved in my own very successful wholesale and retail selling career, as well as through the many people I have trained all over the United States, Mexico, and Puerto Rico— that my integrated system works and is fun to do. Part of that integration is indeed reciprocation with consumers.

When you achieve Mutual Interchange with consumers, they'll trust and confide in you. When they're satisfied by your sincerity, consumers will want to buy from you. Not only because you'll help them, but also because THEY WANT TO HELP YOU TOO! Is this a mutual admiration society? Maybe not, but the kinship will foster loyalty. If you're loyal to your consumers, they'll be the most important things to you, consumers for life.

Loyal consumers deliver a continuity to the business you have and help deliver referral business (from which you have the opportunity to make consumers for life as well). A growing list of consumers gives you a dominant consumer franchise. This is where the rubber meets the road as far as selling more than anybody else goes, and doing it with a higher margin of profit because you don't have to cut prices as much. If you're on commission, having consumers for life maximizes your commission rates. It also makes the business you represent more profitable.

The consumer is happier when this happens too. Far and away, the consumers I interviewed were happier long term, whatever they bought, than when they did NOT under buy from a benefit standpoint. Those who bought on price and gave up benefits were less happy. It's an overworked phrase, but the consumer getting what they want long term is really a win-win-win situation. Your company wins, you win, and the consumer wins.

Making the company you represent more profitable is important. If you own the business, it goes without saying that the healthier your company is, the better off you are as an owner or investor. For others it means something different. There are many very successful salespeople who are great on the retail floor or in the field, who have don't have the desire, skill set, or courage to be their own proprietor. Others simply don't want the additional responsibility. Still, it's important to keep solvent the business that supplies you with leads, has the brick and mortar, advertising, warehousing, warranty, research and engineering, manufacturing, and distribution expense. It allows a good salesperson to be an entrepreneur and enjoy all the resources available without having to risk any of the expense. That's a major contributing factor to the wealth of the best salespeople. They enjoy the high income without the costs involved. Nice work if you can get it, huh?

You must genuinely work to benefit the consumer or client and to convince them of your trustworthiness. For many, the purchase of expensive high–end brown goods (stereos, big screen or plasma televisions), furniture, white goods (major appliances), cabinetry, automobiles, and especially housing will be the biggest purchase they will ever make. These items represent industries with which the average consumer is neither experienced nor well versed. There is natural fear that if they make a mistake with their purchase they will be out a lot of cash and that is of course understandable, as you and I feel the same way.

Trust is paramount and must be worked on from the very beginning. I will talk much more about how to attain this early in the sale in Chapter 4: "Greeting the Consumer." That's where trust starts and it keeps growing in intensity during the Sales Whisperer™ process.

Once we have attained that trust we must never abuse it. At that point, we're obligated to lead consumers into making an informed buying decision, rather than being "sold" something. If they're "sold" something that fails to satisfy their true bottom-line need, you'll get no repeat business from them and certainly no referral business. Repeat and referral business are at the heart of what you must accomplish as a professional salesperson if you want to make the big bucks that selling can afford you for your efforts. After all, if you're going to do this as a profession, you may as well be viewed by your peers and consumers as the best—and make the money that goes along with it. A selling professional has to admit the big money is great; but, like a professional gambler, winning the game is the real adrenalin rush and I love winning.

Principle #2: Entrusting

This simply means that, very early in the process, you identify what the true bottom-line benefits are for your consumers— individualized to them and their family. You may talk about the very same favorite features you always talk about to all consumers or clients, but you "customize" the benefits of those features to the individuals in question. Your favorite ten features may provide you sixty or seventy benefits. It all depends on which ones you need to reach out and grab in order to exceed the expectations of your consumer.

When I say features, it could be features on a product or features of your service. It doesn't matter. Your best features will give you the ammunition to garner maybe 100 benefits—whatever it is the consumer needs. This isn't possible, though, unless you really take the time to ask the proper questions in the beginning, covered in detail in Chapter 5: "The Power of Asking Qualifying (Discovery) Questions." Asking the right questions helps ensure that you have virtually everything you need to close the sale—even before the normal close attempt occurs.

Specify exactly what benefits the consumer (retail or wholesale) wants, when they want them delivered, and get early agreement that if you meet or exceed these expectations they will buy or give you the purchase order today.

The key here is for you to keep the consumer or buyer confirming, each and every time that you identify all of their bottom-line benefits, that you can deliver them affordably and in a timely manner with great terms. Just like the rote learning that programmed us in the first few years of school, repetition programs the consumer or buyer to say yes to the next question. After you program them with a series of questions to which they've answered yes, consumers will find it difficult to say no to you when you ask for the order

This is pressure that you "orchestrate," not pressure you apply. The orchestrated pressure makes the consumers or buyers put pressure on themselves. So pressure is indeed in play here, but PEOPLE DO NOT FEEL PRESSURE FROM YOU. This is particularly effective when you're working with a consumer who has trouble making a decision.

When you ask the proper questions, you'll earn a spot in their hearts that will later earn their money a spot in your pocket or cash register. Not because you put something over on them, though. Au contraire. It's because you rightfully earned their trust and did not betray that trust, delivering all of the benefits they told you they wanted—not what you presumed was important to them.

That's a very key point. By asking the right questions, and then asking follow-up questions based on their answers, until you're sure you get all of the bottom-line benefits, you hardly ever run the risk of wasting time and losing control of the sale. It's easy, after talking to many consumers, to say to yourself, "I know where they're going with this," and then make a bad assumption, putting yourself out of the power position at least briefly, but perhaps long enough to lose the sale.

Principle #3: Image

People tend to judge themselves and others by physical appearance, professional titles, clothing worn, automobiles driven, and stature of the company you represent.

<u>Physical Appearance</u>: This may not be my leading attribute, and maybe not that of most people, but physical appearance does indeed help initially. You know how it is: everything came easy in high school for the beautiful girls and the good looking, athletic guys. Then there are others (who we all hate), who can have pancakes and eggs every morning; a cheeseburger, fries and a piece of pie for lunch; and a big dinner with dessert. They can also have ice cream at night and NEVER PUT ON A POUND! You just want to strangle them, don't you? People who are tall and slender engender respect even when they do nothing to earn it.

The good thing about those who don't have the advantage of natural good looks is that they can fly under the radar and surprise people. Consumers will never see you coming, and by using these techniques, the element of surprise empowers you even more. It's more than a state of mind: when seriously and properly applied, the Sales Whisperer™ techniques have conquered most of the shortcomings of people I have trained.

<u>Title</u>: It's true that an impressive title has clout with consumers and buyers. It implies that you're a decision maker and probably have the power and the resources to

negotiate deals. It's more impressive if you're the Vice-President, Director, or National Sales Manager than if you're "just" a salesperson or company representative. This lack of a title can be overcome.

Handling yourself in a professional, sincere manner, and proving that you're creative and have their best interest at heart can make the difference, and very quickly. Like I said before, not being as good looking as you would like can be overcome if addressed in the right way—but it does have to be overcome. It's just another hurdle you have to jump in order to make the sale. Your focus should be on minimizing the hurdles (and not having an impressive title is one). It can be done very easily with the techniques in this book. It's important that you recognize hurdles and prepare to overcome them.

Pittsburgh Steeler quarterback Charlie Batch once said, "Proper preparation prevents poor performance." That says it all in five words. Lack of a title can be a real roadblock, but it doesn't have to be a deal breaker unless we choose to let it—and no salesperson worth his or her salt will let it. You know the problem exists. Deal with it properly and you can resolve it quickly.

Clothing: Most people perceive professional quality by the way you dress. If someone is particularly well dressed, it makes them look wealthy, successful, intelligent, and in control. A salesperson is always in front of the public and you should always take pride in the way you coordinate your clothing, regardless of how much, or how little, it costs. You don't always have to spend a lot of money to look well groomed and successful. Clean and pressed is the most important part, even if business casual is the norm. Creases in the shirts and slacks mean a lot, as does a shine on the shoes. At the very least, it demonstrates a certain pride you take in yourself and in your profession.

If possible, you should always dress slightly above the required standard so that you can be reasonably sure that you'll be dressed slightly above your consumers or clients.

If you cannot pay more for your attire, make sure you're at least very stylish in how you put your ensemble together. Even if you're short, overweight, or both, you can still dress with style.

And please don't be naive enough to think it goes unnoticed by your consumers, because it certainly does not! You get credit for showing some class and people like to deal with and associate themselves with class. Class doesn't necessarily cost money but it does ALWAYS show pride. It can do part of the selling job for you. You only get one chance at a first impression and a bad or mediocre one creates yet another hurdle. Avoid this one and you won't have to overcome it. Don't let it happen. Work hard to prevent the avoidable and unnecessary hurdles. Even one rock in your wagon makes your load heavier. Unload this one immediately and make your job easier.

Automobiles: People say you must be successful if you drive a Cadillac, Lexus, Acura, Lincoln, BMW, Mercedes Benz, or other luxury car. You've heard that yourself, right? Unfortunately, in some cases this is correct. As with clothes, a clean well-maintained car shows pride and a sense of class and sensibility in a salesperson. In retail, this may not come into play, as the consumer may not ever see your car. In real estate, it's another matter. Still, a sensibility can be perceived if you take "pride in your ride."

Stature of Company: This intangible is a mainstay in successful sales. The reputation of your company is very important in the eyes of the consumer, just as it is in your eyes when you shop. This is why you should parlay this into a power position. If your company is in front of the public with advertising and/or storefronts, it may bring footsteps to you. How you handle them is up to you. The most successful professionals know how to take advantage of this. This isn't an expense that comes out of your pocket, but rather a tool you can use to make these resources even more powerful than they appear.

If you're selling for a store, realtor, or manufacturer, take pride in the paycheck you get on a regular basis. If you're on commission, you earn every penny of it. I know from my experience selling straight commission that this is true. If you're like me, nobody drives your harder than you drive yourself. I respect you for it, but you can also help yourself by working SMARTER and eradicating all the hurdles possible BEFORE you start working harder. Remember the stature of your company, embrace it, and sell it, and you will make your job a little easier.

Every company has its strong and weak points. Your opportunity is to strengthen your position with the consumer or client by itemizing the top five reasons to buy from your company, and also to itemize the additional reasons they should buy from YOU in particular. If you cannot or will not do this, your company doesn't need you. They can find someone else who can do it better. If your company has not provided you with these reasons, it's your job to assure your own success over the average salesperson: research, develop, and promote such a list, and use it with your consumers or clients.

Some of those reasons may also apply to your competitor, but here's the kicker. Many competitors' salespeople are too lazy or not smart enough to develop such a list (thank you very much). If a consumer talks to you (before or after they talk to your competitor) and you can proudly list reasons they should do business with you, and the competitors don't, then some of the strengths your company shares with the competitor become your EXCLUSIVE features. Many consumers or clients will assume the competition doesn't have them or they would have been talking about them too.

When the sale reaches a critical mass these perceived advantages, whether exclusive or not, can make all the difference. Remember what I said earlier: We're playing the percentages in sales. If you want your close rate to improve, you must do three things. One is actually know what your close rate is. Don't guess at it, please. Measure yourself for a month and see where your actual starting point is. It's impossible to track your progress, or lack thereof, unless you know where you started.

The second thing is to use every viable advantage you can. One advantage you have just learned is to use your company's and your own strengths in a way most of your competitors don't. As the old saying goes, "Use it or lose it!" Use it please. The stature of your company is important if you use it right, but your own stature and the advantages you personally afford the consumer are even more important. Use them to your advantage.

The third thing is know your product. It is one of the most important traits missing in most of the salespeople I train. Many of your clients read consumer magazines religiously when anticipating a purchase. I would think it would be embarrassing to salespeople that the consumer sometimes knows more about the product than they do. Apparently, that isn't embarrassing enough for some salespeople because they continue to commit the same mistake!

I bought a car not too long ago. Immediately the salesperson wanted me to negotiate price. If she had listened to what I was saying and took me to a car that fit my needs and then proved to me that all my dreams would be fulfilled by purchasing it, I would have bought from her. I went to another dealership and the salesperson again happened to be a woman. She explained all the features and how they worked. She reminded me of the newspaper article proclaiming that her company had the best service after the sale and the best service department.

She did not knock any other brand of car I was considering, but did have a working knowledge of the competitive cars in this price range. She focused on the strengths she was offering. Strengths that may not have been exclusive to her company, but she was the only one talking about them.

Her technique could have used some polishing, but she definitely had done some homework and I appreciated that. While it took the sales manager to close the deal, I give a lot of the credit to the salesperson because this woman had

PREPARED to SELL. (For what it was worth, I commended her in front of her boss for that effort.) All automobiles are created equal. Because she could speak intelligently about the car versus the competitive model, and because she sold me on the BENEFITS of buying from HER, I bought. I could have negotiated that same deal at almost any dealership that had the same car in inventory. SHE made the difference. I bought from HER.

If the three most important rules of retail truly are location, location, and location (and they are), then the fourth most important rule, in my experience, is that the salesperson must be smart and professional enough to use all of his or her available resources. Do it. Do it now and you'll be happier and more successful!

In short, titles, clothing, automobiles, the stature of your company and product are important to consider in professional selling, but you are most the important element. You can make the consumer defer to your opinion and even gain obedience (submission) from them if you execute the techniques properly. You now know how to do that. I hope you're now starting to say, "Put me in coach, I want to play"!

Principle #4: Safety in Numbers

A saying popular in the 1980s was "Nobody gets fired for buying IBM." This is the "everybody's doing it" theory. It simply means that it really helps to give the consumer or buyer experience they don't possess, experience based on what others are doing or have done.

It has been said by many that 95% of people are imitators and only 5% initiators. People are persuaded more by the actions of others than any sales proof you can offer. You may think this is profound, but not new. It is new! It's new to a lot of people. It's new to people who have known it but fail to use it effectively and religiously. This is a very powerful tool and the salespeople who use it prove it constantly. All of the consumers with which you deal are human. (Despite what we might think about some of the consumers we've dealt with.)

So talk about your past consumers who had the same or similar wants and needs (benefits), and talk about how you exceeded their expectations. I've met very few consumers (even buyers) who could intelligently differentiate between want and need. Most consumers I've run into, particularly at retail, just cannot separate them. That's your cue to continue being in control by helping them understand the difference. The easiest way to do that is to concentrate on the bottom-line benefit I talked about earlier. I'll talk much more about this in Chapter 6: "Feature-Function-Benefit Selling," and Chapter 7: "Handling Consumer Objections."

Principle #5: Follow Me

Commonly held tenets of this are called by different names, but for me they're easy to remember as Keeping Up With the Jones', Association, and Praise.

Keeping up with the Jones': Consumers love it when they can associate themselves with people they respect by purchasing a similar product or moving into the same neighborhood. For example, if you're selling a home you could say (if truthful), "A lot of ABC and XYZ company execs live in this neighborhood." This tells the consumer that smart successful people have chosen this neighborhood and that they would be safe to choose it too.

Association: People like to do business with people who are similar to them, but who possess a particular expertise that they don't possess. When consumers meet a salesperson who is similar to them but possesses the appropriate expertise, they become compliant, and enter into the very thing you want in a selling situation—a calm and submissive state. This is the ultimate badge of trust and you cannot and should not ever betray that trust.

Common sense should tell you never to talk down to anyone whose pocket you're trying to get into; but alas, not all salespeople are professionals and they make that mistake. Those salespeople (and I use the word loosely), give a poor reputation to the sales industry. The good news is that people always have to buy from somebody, and if you talk on the consumer's level, you win. Winning is victory. It brings you a higher remuneration for your efforts and stronger promotion opportunities. In addition, having a reputation as the best in your store, best of your outside sales force, or simply the best in class is a wonderful feeling, and worth the effort.

Praise: This is a difficult one. It's not easy to shower your consumer or client with praise (even though they love to hear it) because it's almost expected. Consumers and buyers are also savvy enough to recognize this as pandering and shameless when they get it from salespeople who really don't believe it or care. Because this happens every day to many people in many places, it predisposes them for a rather cool reception to praise. Offer praise only when you're confident that you have the consumer in that calm, submissive state you worked for early in the greeting and questioning parts of the sale (covered in more detail in Chapter 4: "Greeting the Consumer," and Chapter 5: "The Power of Asking Qualifying (Discovery) Questions").

Principle #6: Limited Time/Insufficient Supply

The harder something is to get, the more people want it! You can use this technique on most people, but for maximum effectiveness, you must first gain their trust (covered in detail in the Greeting and Questioning chapters). When presented in the right manner and at the right time—which is NOT at the beginning of the sales presentation—this can be an extremely persuasive tool in your arsenal. Use it too early and the average consumers will suspect a lying salesperson's trick to get them to buy.

Unfortunately, there are salespeople out there who choose not to polish their skills and master their craft. But if you've chosen to do so, this affords you the opportunity to prove to the consumer or client, based on how you handle yourself and on your timing when using this technique, that they are in fact dealing with the right person.

In my experience, people don't get excited about Spring Flings or George Washington's birthday sales. They look for a legitimate reason to believe that NOW is the time to buy, as opposed to shopping around for a while. Make sure that your reasons for buying today are factual and legitimate, and use real life scenarios such as, "Our floor plan (wholesale financing) is due in three days and we need to turn the product NOW." Or, "I'm trying to win a sales contest and I'm doing almost anything to win." That makes sense to the consumer. It creates urgency for the consumer to buy now. While more of this will be covered in Chapter 8: "Closing the Sale," some other examples of Limited Time/Insufficient Supply are, "The sale ends Saturday"; "We only have a few of these close-outs left"; and, "The favorable financing is only available for two more days."

Get the picture?

It's human nature to want the very thing that we're denied, or to want the goods or services that are in short supply. When you offer a premium or benefit to consumers to entice them to buy, it's like a cushy carpet under their feet. Just as they're basking in the glow and comfort of getting in on a deal, you—in effect, and with great vigor—threaten to pull the rug out from under them if they don't buy now.

This technique can be used very effectively but you never, ever use it early in the selling encounter. Use it only as a trial close (talked about later), and only after you've explained the benefits and start to get positive buying signals from the consumer.

I believe that 95% of consumer decision making occurs subconsciously. (That's a lot of decisions over which we have no conscious control!) If 95% of consumer decision making occurs subconsciously, this may be why the Limited Time/

Insufficient Supply technique is so effective when you use it honestly and convincingly. *Blink: The Power of Thinking without Thinking*, by Malcolm Gladwell (Little, Brown, 2005), talks at length about the split-second, subconscious decisions that we all make each day. I highly recommend you purchase his book and read it to gain insight into how people's first impressions color their decision making.

I also highly recommend that you finish this book and put into practice the Sales Whisperer™ system. Shameless self-promotion, you say? Nah, you already spent the money for the book. The psychology works. Use it, be successful, and make me proud of you.

Chapter 2

How People Learn

Understanding how people learn and process information is an extremely valuable tool in determining whether your information is getting through to your consumer or buyer. You can also use it to help you get a job you're interviewing for or when you're interviewing someone else.

You cannot sell anything, be it a product, service, idea, concept—or even yourself—unless you can recognize a consumer's "hot buttons." (And let's face it, even if you're interviewing for a job, you're selling. You're selling yourself and your value to the potential employer.) Knowing what to watch for and when to watch it is vital to the selling scenario.

You've heard that men and women are different, right? It's true that while they share a commonality in many respects, inbred or cultivated through life experiences, there are still innate, sometimes subtle differences that can make or break a selling situation. We need to be cognizant of what these differences are and what they mean if we want to attain and maintain control of the selling situation. If we miss something, it could lead to an objection, which is dangerous. If that happens we can get to the very end of the transaction and find that something we thought was important to our consumer isn't that big a deal, and that we missed elaborating on something that is important. Worse yet, the buyers, consumers, or interviewers might not even raise their questions or objections. It may mean that we did not hit all of their "hot buttons," and maybe wasted our time and theirs, elaborating on something that was not really all that important to them.

With that in mind, we need to learn and practice how to enter people's minds by learning what they think, why they think it, and why men and women hear and process information differently. Remember the Las Vegas scenario I mentioned earlier, about stacking the odds in our favor? We need to do that again. There are certain things we can watch for in our consumers that will help us gain and maintain control of the selling situation.

All people learn through their senses. The latest survey I did showed that 83% of people learn by sight. In my symposiums I say, "83% of people learn and tend to process information by what they see. Not ALL people, but most people. WOMEN tend to learn—not all women, but most women—tend to learn…" and then I insert a strategic pause. I look around the room, watching the women, and then say, "By SIGHT." Even before I pause, almost every woman lifts her eyes from her note taking and looks at me, fearing or interested in what I'm going to say next. I get these looks like, "What is he going to say about women? What's he know about a woman?"

Well, the truth is, even though I'm married to a woman and have two daughters and a granddaughter, what I know about women you could put in a thimble; however, I do know a couple of important things. I know how women tend to think and how they tend to process information, and how that affects the selling process. Again, during the strategic pause nearly every woman—even if she is taking notes or talking to the person next to her—stops what she is doing and looks up at me. That's it—they look dead at me to see if I'm going to make real sense or, possibly, a disparaging remark.

Women tend to learn by what they see. They want to hear what you have to say, but it's very important to most of them that they see you and see how you say it. What I was about to share was important because I was going to say something about women and they wanted to hear it. When I remind them that most of them immediately looked at me when I started to talk about women, they understand. And when I point out that they could have had a different reaction but that most did not, they cannot argue: they looked at me. Then they give me an understanding and knowing smile.

Remember: most women tend to learn and process information by their sense of sight. What does this tell you when you're selling to or interviewing with a woman? Why is this important? When I ask these questions in my seminars, everyone, even the men, understands the concept. With most women, the eyes really are the pathway to what they're thinking and reveal what is important to them.

How do we use this in sales? When they're interested in what you're talking about, most women will give you constant eye contact. If they start looking around (like some girls did when I was asking for a date in my adolescence), they're not interested in what you're saying. This means two significant things. One, you need to change to another subject that you perceive is interesting to them and two, in the questioning process you did not do a good enough job of uncovering their true bottom-line benefits.

All I can say is shame on us if we let that happen. Get angry when this happens if you want, but channel that anger toward yourself because you were the one that didn't do effective enough detective work on the front end.

While the Sales Whisperer™ technology is an integrated program, it's heavily weighted toward the front end of the selling process. While putting the consumer in a calm, submissive frame of mind by asking fact-finding or discovery questions, we should be uncovering everything we need to know in order to close the sale. We should spend more time asking qualifying questions than we do presenting the product.

Salespeople (me included) tend to be outspoken extroverts who think out loud and want to dominate the conversation.

In my opinion, this is the biggest error we can make. We need the discipline to listen intelligently to what a woman says and formulate questions from her answers until we're sure we have clearly identified the bottom-line benefit. But—and this is just as important—we need to watch a woman's eyes to ensure we're getting our message across.

By this point in my seminars, the men are all smiling. Some say they wish they had known this when they were dating, or that they'll try to use it to their advantage now with their wives or girlfriends. One interesting thing about having this knowledge about women is we can make our job of selling more fun to do.

I have found that most women (remember: not all, but most) even talk in the same manner as they learn:

"Oh, I **SEE** what you're saying."

"I'm getting a mental **PICTURE** of that right now."

"I can **ENVISION** how that would look in my family room."

Don't laugh out loud or even smile when you hear a woman say this. Smile on the inside if you must, that makes it fun. But what else does this tell you? These are buying signs and it's time for a trial close. (I will cover specific techniques in Chapter 8: "Closing the Sale.") When interviewing for a job, this is the time to say, "When would you like me to start?"

Now, get ready men: it's your turn. The study said 11% of people learn by hearing. They're auditory learners. I say to my group, "MEN tend to learn and process information through (strategic pause)…what they HEAR." During that strategic pause, I look at as many men in the room as I can, and most of them have their heads turned slightly toward me. About a third of the time I see a man who is sitting to my right or left turn his opposite ear toward me…a most uncomfortable position. I say, "You've totally done a 'Linda Blair' move to hear me." I then ask, "Are you right or left ear dominant?" When they admit they turned what would be the wrong ear toward me, my point to the group is made.

So how can you tell if a man is interested in what you're

saying? Men tend to turn their dominant ear toward you when they think something important or interesting is about to be said—just as they did during my strategic pause. I'm not talking about a violent jerk that makes his head roll off his shoulders and fall to the floor; it's a subtle turn you need to watch for when talking to a man.

Do men also talk the way they think? You bet they do. How many times have you heard one guy say to another, "I **HEAR** you man"?

You'll also hear them frequently say:

"I **HEARD** that."

"If I **HEAR** you correctly, you're saying…"

"It **SOUNDS** to me you're saying…"

These are all buying signals telling you a trial close is in order. Once again, keep your composure and smile on the inside, but recognize that the sale has been or is close to being made. Don't take a chance of talking until you've talked your way out of the sale. Try a trial close.

At this point a woman will say something like, "Wait a minute! If only 11% of people learn by hearing and most men learn that way, then that explains why men simply don't learn!" (This also seems to be my wife's theory.) How does one argue with that? My first impulse is to just say what I say at home, which is, "Yes dear," but my experience allows me to go on to explain that some men (not most) learn by sight, making them visual learners, and that some women (not most) learn by hearing and are auditory learners.

We're playing the percentages again here. We're simply stacking the odds in our favor. The best we can do is roll the dice and know that most women tend to learn by sight and that most men tend to learn (if they do learn) by what they hear.

But what is always true is that professional salespeople will listen, watch, and interpret what they hear and see.

In case you're interested in how the rest of the world learns, 3.5% of people learn by smell, and yes, they tend to talk that way too. As in: "I can **SMELL** the excitement in the air."

1.5% of people learn by touch. In my experience, these tend to be the people taking copious notes during my seminars. They feel that if they don't write everything down they'll miss something. When I notice people taking a lot of notes I interact with them in a way that fits the way they learn: I write salient points on a white board or provide them with collateral materials, such as handouts. Consumers who take notes while talking to you are the ones who need to touch the product you're selling. Have them hold parts of the product while you point out features and sell their benefits.

As for the final 1% of the population, they learn by (are you ready for this?) taste! They actually think they learn something from taste and yes, they sometimes talk this way as in "This idea has a delicious **FLAVOR** to it." (Go figure.)

I have demonstrated these findings time after time in my seminars. Most women react exactly as I described above, by looking directly at me. Most men turn their dominant ear toward me. I've never had anyone question the validity of the information I shared because they all saw it happen to each other live! This is usually one of the most light-hearted and humorous segments of my presentations, but for the rest of our time together, the participants are much more cognizant and vocal about how they react to things they see and hear. You be cognizant too, please.

Chapter 3

Preparing to Sell

One important element in selling is the ability to prepare to sell. Selling is a profession like any other, and to be the best at what you do in any field, you need to prepare yourself mentally in order to achieve the success you desire. There are many salespeople out there but not many true professionals. The best of the best follow a routine each day before they actually meet the consumer. If you'll permit me to use a sports analogy, the best golfers in the world go through a pre-shot routine. All professional athletes have a preparation routine.

Leave your personal life at home

We're all human. Sometimes we oversleep. We might go to our car and discover a flat tire that makes us late for work. We may have just had an argument with our spouse. We could be having a bad hair day, or just not feel on top of our game. The thing you must remember is that the consumer really doesn't care about any of that.

Consumers and buyers have their own problems. Everything that can happen to you can also happen to them. Consumers have enough to worry about in their own lives and they just don't care about your problems. They don't want to hear about them, and they don't want to have a negative experience because you're having a bad day. They have their own issues to think about and today, their problem should be your priority.

Particularly in retail, consumers come to you because they have a problem, one that's going to cost them some of their hard-earned money to solve. Money that they may or may not have planned to spend, and money that they had not put away in anticipation of having to replace something. They're often afraid that it's going to cost them much more money than the last time they bought or replaced the item in question. When they come through the door, many consumers are thinking that life just isn't fair. A television ought to last more than 18 years! Why can't I get 300,000 miles on my car?

Don't forget that the average consumer is wary of salespeople in general (and some in particular). Many remember negative stories they've heard or actually experienced. You must overcome those fears quickly in order to take control of the sale from the very beginning. I cannot stress enough how important that is.

After you decide to leave your own problems at home (they'll still be there when you return), you must think about what you need to do in your "performance." That's what sales is all about, you know. It's a performance. In order to behave as if you don't have problems, you must put on an act. Like any performer, you must learn to psych yourself up so that you can be "on" during the course of the day. The consumer may be having a bad day too, and needs to know that he or she can lean on you like a friend—without you adding to their woes.

Show confidence

The next thing you need to do while preparing for the day is to remember to show confidence. Confidence shows on your face and in your body language, regardless of what you say or how you say it. Consumers need to believe that you can make their problems go away. They can't do that if they sense that you have problems of your own.

You must remember to stay calm. Never, ever, look or act surprised by something the consumer or client says. The only three things you ever show are a genuine empathy for the consumer's problem, a sense of humor (but always in good taste), and a willingness to provide an intelligent and affordable solution to the problem that brought them to you. After all, they know they have to spend money (and maybe more than they would like) to alleviate their problem and they want to deal with a professional. You must be the one to earn their business versus another salesperson of lesser ability.

I say again, you must remain calm and collected. Make sure that you're the strong, calming force that they need you to be so that you'll be the one to solve their problem—and collect their money.

It's important that you show empathy and an understanding of their problem. Please remember that empathy is putting yourself in the consumer's shoes. Don't confuse empathy with sympathy, which sometimes comes across as condescension. Your voice and body language can project a negative message, even though that's not your intention.

Expect to succeed

The people you deal with can sense this attitude. Without projecting arrogance, you must display a sense of big brotherly or sisterly understanding and compassion. The consumer appreciates a verbal pat on the back. You cannot do it naturally—as it must be done—unless you mentally practice it before you leave the house.

Each of these things can be done in just a few minutes. It takes more time to read this chapter than it will take to get ready for your performance in the morning. It's a ritual you must go through before you hit center stage, just like a professional entertainer would do (and does).

Show enthusiasm

Be enthusiastic about solving the consumers' problems, but in a controlled way. Show a genuine interest in their wants and needs and LISTEN to what they have to say in order to determine the true bottom-line benefits they seek. Don't go overboard, but don't convey boredom while they explain their problem. This isn't always easy to avoid because if you've been selling a while, you will have heard most of the stories before. It's easy to become indifferent to them. You just cannot allow yourself to project that kind of image. Treat every concern as something you've addressed successfully in the past, which makes you the right person to help them make the problem go away, but at the same time, show empathy for their distress.

Again, this is a performance, and you'll be handsomely paid for an award-winning one. Be willing to show humor but remember, always, to turn the humor toward yourself. I'm not talking about a comedic performance that will have them lose confidence in your ability or willingness to help them. Just enough to cut the tension. The next time the consumer has a problem, he or she will think of you first, will come to see another performance, and will be willing to pay for it.

Display leadership

Remember, the consumer isn't an expert in your field with ready access to your product (at least at a wholesale level), and doesn't possess your knowledge about the product, warranty, etc. You simply need to demonstrate, by attitude and words, that you've been here many times before with former consumers, and that you're very good at what you do—which is help them solve their problems. Say, "I understand." That's what leaders do. By saying "I understand" a few times in response to what they say, consumers will derive comfort from the fact that you're actually listening to them. You don't need to elaborate. Simply saying, "I understand," sends the message loud and clear.

If you're a salesperson, you're probably an extrovert like me. We'd rather be talking than listening. That makes this technique very difficult for us to do, but it's oh, so effective for the consumer or buyer. Most salespeople cannot resist the temptation to go off on a tangent or to start selling before they've taken the appropriate time to listen (and I mean really listen) to the consumer, and to ask questions in order to discover that bottom-line benefit.

If you think about this during your morning preparations, it only takes a few seconds to get into that mindset, and then it will come naturally when the rubber really meets the road. That would be within the last three feet of the sale. Three feet is about as close as you get to the consumer without invading their comfort zone.

When you condition yourself to say, "I understand what you're saying, and I've faced this problem with my consumers many times before," you will garner the consumer's respect and submissiveness. You'll remain in control of the sales process.

Review the reasons why consumers should do business with your company

We talked about this in Chapter 1. As part of your morning preparation, mentally review the five reasons a consumer should do business with your company in general and with you in particular. This keeps them fresh in your mind so that they'll roll off your tongue in an easy, natural way when you need to play that trump card. It may seem old hat to you, reciting a list of the same reasons to every consumer, but remember that this is the first time they've heard it from you—and very possibly the first time they've heard it anywhere. This information acts as a "pre-close," and lowers the possibility of an objection later. They may even be inclined to close the sale themselves.

Review your closers

Next, review your closers for the day. Remember what specials you can talk about, such as sale pricing, extending 0% free financing, and free delivery and installation for the retail consumer. For a company's buyer you might extend floor planning terms or pre-paid freight. Maybe you have closeouts or market development funds for incremental advertising opportunities or co-op from your company.

Once again, practice and preparation will enable you to orchestrate smooth transitions in your selling presentation.

Set your objectives

Finally, set your own personal objectives for the month, week, and day and review them each morning. Be aware of the quota you've set for yourself (or that your boss has set for you—ugh!), and start thinking about what you must do to accomplish it. Remember, without objectives you have nothing definitive for which to aim. Also, remember that an objective is different from a goal. A goal is a nice thing to do. An objective is something you have to achieve, such as making a certain number of closes for the day. Your objective will be a little different for a day, a week, or a month but there should be an objective for each.

Develop sound objectives:

- Make them specific to what you want to accomplish. If you're a furniture salesperson and have an assigned quota—that you have to sell a certain number of recliners each month—you may want to set an objective that you'll bring up the subject of recliners to every consumer you talk to that day.

- Make your objectives measurable—for example, how many recliners you'll sell during the month and what you need to sell each day in order to meet your quota. "I must sell three recliners each day." That can be measured. At the end of the day, ask yourself, "Did I sell at least three recliners today?"

- Your objectives must be achievable. Break the quota down by the day so that you can attack it in bite-sized chunks rather than trying to sell one consumer 67 recliners on the last day of the month!

- Objectives must be relevant. Are they individualized to you and your business? If you're expected to sell service policies on all your products, an objective to sell a minimum number of service policies is indeed relevant.

- Objectives must be time-bound. What do you have to do to satisfy your daily quota? Did you sell the needed amount by the end of the day? Did you sell enough in the morning to achieve your objective, or did it take all day? Were you short two sales? Did you sell more than you needed to in the given time frame?

If you set proper objectives, you'll know specifically what you need to sell, you can measure the actual amount sold versus your objective, and you know that the objective was achievable or realistic. Further, you identified the relevancy of the objective and set a time frame in which to get the stuff sold and out the door. The more precise the objective, the more control you have in delivering positive results in your efforts to achieve.

Remember: preparing to sell should be a regular part of your daily routine.

- Leave your personal life at home.
- Show confidence.
- Expect to succeed.
- Prepare to show enthusiasm.
- Display leadership.
- Review the five reasons a consumer should buy from you.
- Review your closers.
- Set objectives.

Now you're ready to greet the consumer.

Chapter 4

Greeting the Consumer

**Perception: Sales are won or lost at the end of the sale.
Reality: Sales are won or lost at the beginning of the sale.**

I talked to one salesperson long ago about his initial contact with a consumer. He said that when he "approached" the consumer he did certain things. I thought, "Huh?!" We don't "approach" a consumer; we "approach" wild animals in the zoo. We don't approach consumers as if there was any imminent danger. Professional salespeople don't lurk in the shadows waiting to pounce on consumers as a lion would on his prey.

People sense our fear just as we sense theirs, and even thinking "approach" instead of "greet" forces you to demonstrate a body language that is not conducive to obtaining someone's trust. Today the public has way too many shopping places from which to choose. The consumer really does have choices, after all, and you want them to be glad they chose you.

You have to put them at ease right away in order to put them into that calm, submissive state so that, rather than selling them something, you can guide them into making an informed buying decision. Let consumers know that you appreciate them by acknowledging and greeting them as they come through the door. Even if you're with other consumers, say "Hello," or "Welcome," and that you'll be with them soon.

You might even say, "I guess you heard about our big sale too! I'll be with you shortly." This is a control statement. It's a way of reassuring consumers that they're in the right place and that it will be worth the wait.

As I said earlier, don't approach consumers like wild animals, but rather greet them like friends. When you're free to do so, walk toward them at a natural pace, a sincere smile on your face—just as you would a friend. This promotes a non-confrontational attitude and makes consumers feel welcome. After all, the store spends a lot of money on advertising (maybe 2-4% of net revenue) trying to get footsteps through the door, and when consumers cooperate by coming in you should greet them warmly. But don't do what the consumer expects—which is that you will walk quickly toward them, tongue hanging out and drool dripping off of it, with your hand outstretched even when you're still halfway across the room. (Well okay, that's an exaggeration, but that's what some consumers I have interviewed said.)

Try this instead: smile and walk naturally toward them and say something you thought of earlier in the day when you were at home or in your car, preparing to sell.

If it's raining hard or steady you can say, for example, "If you came in to get dry, welcome!" Or, "Wow! How long since you've seen rain like this?"

If it's snowing, you can say, "Welcome. Have you heard how many inches we're supposed to get?"

Another example of an opening statement is, "You must need a new car. Why aren't you out on the golf course on a day like today and why am I not with you?"

Openings like these, when offered with a sincere smile, bring a smile to most consumers' faces. They sound like questions that you might ask a friend who stops by your place of business. That's EXACTLY what you want with your consumer. They don't trust you yet because they still don't know you. You want their first impression to be that you very well may become a friend in whom they can place their trust.

The absolute last thing you want to say is, "Can I 'help' you?" The consumer switches to autopilot and says, "No thanks, I'm just looking." You've failed to take control of the situation, and have created an additional hurdle that you must overcome in order to assume control.

Relax the consumer. Remember, you want them in a calm, submissive state. Make your opening statement humorous, as in the examples above. Consumers will be more at ease and respond more openly if you show them a little humor and talk in a calm, friendly manner. There is no psychological principle that states that you lose respect and control of the consumer if you show a little humor.

In fact, many psychologists believe that humor increases retention of information, which augments the weapons we possess to assist consumers into that calm and submissive state more rapidly. (Hey, maybe we should ask them to lie down on the couch...nah, that's psychiatry!) If you use opening statements to break the ice, a person overhearing your selling presentation might mistake your consumer for an old fishing partner.

Unfortunately, when most people think of salespeople, one of the first images to come to mind is someone on commission working on an "UP" system. In the UP system, salespeople are on a rotation. After they work with a consumer, they go to the back of the line. Whether they close or not, they go to the back of the line. When they are next "up," they know that they must make a sale because, close or not, they go to the back of the rotation. They must make the most of each opportunity to make money and will generally do anything to make the sale.

While this system isn't very popular anymore—because it makes salespeople too aggressive and consumers don't like it—the memories still linger. The UP system does not promote the image of a professional who is genuinely interested in getting consumers the right product, with the correct benefits, customized to their individual needs. It perpetuates, instead, the perception that all sales are about the salesperson and not about solving the consumers' problems. Unfortunately, many fast-track stores and automotive lots still use the UP system.

Joe Panzica

Remember, as I said before, consumers generally have an unanticipated problem, and they're going to have to spend money not earmarked for that problem. How many people do you know who put money away every month just in case they have to replace their computer, refrigerator, or furnace? Some people might budget savings for something sexier like a big screen TV or an automobile, but even then, more often than not they end up spending more than they anticipated.

I have encountered very few people who came into my place of business and said, "Hello Joe, I'm Scott. PLEASE take my money!" Remember this, and put yourself in their shoes, showing the same empathy you would want if you were the one with an unexpected problem for which you had to shell out your hard-earned cash to solve the problem.

Without being condescending, project an image (whether it's inside sales or not) that you are not a salesperson in the normal sense (whatever normal is). The image you want to project is that of a professional who can, through verbal examination, diagnose the problem—much like a physician—and prescribe the product or service that will make the consumer well. The appropriate product or service, of course, will deliver all the benefits that are important to them.

Remember, regardless of how smart consumers or buyers may be in their own field, they're in your world now, and you typically know much more about what is available to alleviate their problems and concerns than they do. Approach this whole "vignette," if you will (remember, you're performing a role), with a little bit of compassion. It's almost as if you're saying, "I understand; don't be afraid; you've come to the right person and I know how to make it all better." Don't ham it up too much with this, but it's a very effective approach to take with the consumer. Whether they admit it or not, they are not informed enough in your industry to make 100% quality choices without your professional guidance.

First and foremost, open with a smile. A smile is contagious. The majority of people will smile back, even if it's a micro-expression they try to hold back. A micro-expression is an involuntary response that the consumer may not be aware of, but which expresses his or her true feelings. (Adelson 2004) We will talk more about micro-expressions in Chapter 12: "Some Proven Ways to Suspect Lies," but for now be aware that even a micro-expression is a clue that they appreciated and are at least a little relaxed by your friendly expression. This helps relieve the normal pressure felt by someone coming into a new and unfamiliar environment.

Always extend your hand to shake theirs. Regardless of what you may have heard, when somebody wants to conduct business with you, he or she expects to be treated with respect and in a businesslike manner, and that includes a handshake. The handshake should be firm in the beginning—but not as if you're arm wrestling. Match the grip of the consumer or client. When I get the dead fish handshake, I just lighten my grip. When shaking hands with a man, be sure to pull away first, giving his hand a small squeeze as you do. This reinforces your leadership position.

What about shaking hands with a woman? The answer is definitely! Far and away, most women I talk to say they want a handshake, just like a man. They say they spend the same money and want the same respect, and I think that is true and understandable. So how do you shake a woman's hand? Just like a man's. Extend your hand slowly and maintain a three-foot distance between the two of you. Use a firm but not overly hard grip and adjust to the firmness you receive from her.

Never squeeze a woman's hand before releasing it, as you would a man's hand. Simply match her grip and then let go. And never, in a business environment, should you cup your other hand over hers as you might with a relative. This is far too personal and very un-businesslike. Remember, people will get an initial impression from your handshake just as you do from theirs. Giving the dead fish handshake can be the kiss of death. Make sure you don't do it.

During this time, humanize yourself in their eyes. Show

that you're professional yet approachable, and willing to assist them in any way you can. Shake hands firmly, tell them your name, and ask for theirs. Thank them for considering your store, and ask if one of your consumers referred them. If you can, find out what made them visit. (It's nice to know if your advertising is working.) Write the names down and use their first names—like a friend would—during the conversation. Most people are flattered to hear their first name and respond positively to it. In my experience, when you use consumers' names, they're more likely to remember what you say. I always use consumers' names.

The other reason to use a person's name is so you don't forget it. More than once early in my career, I spent 25 minutes acting like a friend and convincing consumers to buy from me. They used my name a few times and I realized I had forgotten theirs. I tried to remember, but I was too dumb. I closed the sale at $1,850 plus tax, and then the embarrassment commenced. I wrote up the ticket and said (cleverly), "Will you spell your last name please?" After they said, "G-R-E-E-N," I recovered and said, "Of course, I meant that I did not know if you spelled it with an 'e' on the end or not!"

Then I had to say, "I'm sorry, I forgot your first name, what is it again?" I had just convinced this couple to purchase something at $400 more than they wanted to spend and couldn't even remember the man's name. The look on his face said it all. He and his wife had been kidding around with me like friends and they trusted my judgment, and I could not even remember his name. You and I know that you're lucky to have 10 minutes with a retail consumer; I got 25, and could not even show him the respect of remembering his name (or his wife's for that matter). From that moment on I always wrote consumers' names on a small pad of paper I carried.

On a fast-track retail floor, you can try opening with a close, but always do it with a smile. I have opened with, "I can deliver two of these to you Saturday," and the consumer said, "No, but I'll take one." That was it. The consumers had been to another store, which did not have the model they were looking for, and I did. They said my price was a little higher, but I had it in stock. I was busy and had more consumers waiting, so why waste time? This doesn't happen often, but it's great when it does—especially when you're already busy.

If you're in outside sales or calling on a buyer, the same principle about the smile, handshake, and humanizing applies. There's not much to greeting, whether the consumer is visiting you or you them. What matters is that we do it correctly. It sets the tone for the sale, and helps us take control of the selling situation. Control the conversation, and you control the selling situation.

Chapter 5

The Power of Asking Qualifying (Discovery) Questions

This is the most important part of the Sales Whisperer™ method. It will arm you with crucial data that most salespeople never learn about clients. It continues that non-pressure control over your consumer.

Suppose John and Mary Consumer came into your place of business. You smiled, offered an icebreaker, shook their hands, and wrote down their names. It's time to ask some qualifying and fact-finding questions.

Ask permission to ask questions

Always get permission to ask questions of your consumers, and tell them why you're doing it. If you just say, "Do you mind if I ask you a few questions?" they might say something to the effect of, "I'll know what I want when I see it." At this point, you've lost control and must think of a way to get it back. These people don't know you well enough yet to answer your questions blindly.

You need to reassure them that you're not going to ask for their bank PIN. You're not looking for their social security numbers. You don't want to know the ages of their daughters. Try saying, "In order to save you time and money, may I ask you a few questions so I can guide you specifically to the product that will satisfy all your needs?" What's the consumer going to say, "No, I want to waste time and pay as much as humanly possible for this product"? I think not.

Since you explained why you want to ask, as opposed to simply peppering them with questions, odds are high that John and Mary Consumer will understand, say yes, and cooperate. When your reasons are sound, consumers are comfortable talking about themselves. It is, after all, the subject they know the most about. They slip into a more submissive state when they talk about themselves. The same holds true in wholesale selling. Asking questions honors the buyer, and if you exhibit data that you've researched in advance, it's most impressive and they're more apt to give you more time to ask questions.

Asking the right questions, and then asking additional questions based on the consumers' answers until you uncover that true bottom-line benefit, is very powerful.

Let's examine the kinds of questions we ask, and why.

Fact-Finding Questions

This is truly the discovery period. As stated earlier, when done correctly you will get all the information you need to close the sale. You may not even have to ask for the order when you deliver the bottom-line benefits. You cannot deliver them, though, unless you first discover what they are. Every question you ask must be open-ended, and every question you ask must be phrased to elicit a revealing answer.

For example, if you're selling an electric range, you might ask who will be using the oven. (I'll bet no one asked that question down the street.) You might immediately find out that the consumers have an elderly parent living with them, or kids who would use it a little. This allows you to show them a range that has large, easy to read controls— perfect for younger children and elderly folks who have trouble reading. This could be a major benefit that they had not even thought of (and one that the salesperson down the street certainly didn't present).

You should also develop short cuts. Let's stay with major appliances for the time being. You might ask John and Mary Consumer, "How many people in your family?" Let's say that John proudly says, "Five." If you immediately start presenting a super-capacity washer, he might stop you and say, "We don't need anything that big."

Bewildered, you say, "But you said you were washing for five!" Mary Consumer then says, "No, we're washing for two. Two of our kids are away at college, and one is married. We're basically empty-nesters."

You lost control because you didn't keep asking follow-up questions based on their answers. If you had asked, instead, "For how many people will you be washing?" you would have saved time, gotten to the bottom line, and stayed in control.

The moral to the scenario above is to keep asking questions until you're sure that you know the consumers' bottom-line needs. If you can think of a question that will immediately get you that bottom-line answer, use it. I committed a few mistakes early in my career, like the one above, and it embarrassed me. I lost control by proving to the consumer that I wasn't listening, and that I was too eager to get to the close. I promise you, if you spend more time on questions, you'll spend less time on selling, and your close rate will rise dramatically.

On any product that consumers (or buyers in a wholesale situation) are replacing, first ask positive questions about their old product. "What did you like about it?" Or, "What were the features you enjoyed?"

Then ask, "What would you like to improve by getting the new product?"

Sometimes when you ask a negative question like, "What didn't you like about your old product?" the consumer gets a little defensive. Consumers don't want you to think they're dumb and were "sold" something, as opposed to making a wise purchase. Defensiveness puts the consumer on the other side of the fence and you have lost control. Don't take that chance. Keep the questions positive and you'll get the answers you want.

Take notes! If, during the questioning period you unveil five major benefits that the consumer or buyer wants, and they balk at the price later, you need to repeat the five reasons they should buy from you. When you repeat back to them the benefits that they asked for and that you delivered, they realize you remembered them all. Your personal organization may intimidate some of them a little bit initially, but because you listened, they'll respect you for it. Asking questions, with permission, does not irritate consumers. Once they understand the kind of questions you're asking and why, they know that you can help. You can then help them rationalize why they need to pay a few dollars more initially to get everything they told you they needed.

As stated earlier, most consumers don't recognize the difference between want and need. By drilling down to the real benefits needed, you can help them clearly see what they need. Consumers and buyers will pay more for what they need than what they want.

Don't assume that because you've talked to many consumers that the current ones will need the same benefits. Individualize your questions and your subsequent presentation, and it will be much more effective. Ironically, I have found (and former students have seconded this) that the more discovery or fact-finding questions you ask a consumer or buyer, the more trust they afford you.

This is true in a buyer's case only if you show them that you did your homework before you sat down with them. Ask the questions that only they can answer.

When you ask the right fact-finding questions, consumers expect to see fewer choices. They know that you'll only show them an item that will deliver the benefits they need for their particular situation. They feel they can make a decision faster, and they can. They're willing to pay a little more to get a product that delivers all their needs. (Is that a surprise to you?) Consumers really enjoy this type of purchasing experience. This is not only a pleasant purchase experience in their view, but one they would highly recommend to their friends.

Joe Panzica

Feel-Finding Questions

Once you believe that you've gotten all of the true bottom-line benefits necessary to close the sale, you can smile and ask a Feel-Finding Question, such as, "How would you feel if I told you I could show you three models that would give you every benefit YOU TOLD ME was important to you? Would it upset you if I told you all three were on sale?"

What's the consumer going to say? "No, I want products that only fulfill SOME of my needs"? "I was hoping to pay full retail for the product"? Of course you're going to get positive answers. These were non-pressure "control" questions. You continue to control the selling situation.

When the consumer says, "Yes, I would like to see the three models that will give me every benefit I told you I needed," smile and say, "Follow me." Follow me is a command that shows that you're in control. And you are. Consumers follow you at this point because you've listened to their needs and presumed nothing. You've promised to deliver everything they need at a sale price. What's not to love? They'd follow you anywhere!

After you say, "Follow me," turn and LEAD them to the aforementioned three models (or whatever product it is that will fulfill their bottom-line benefits). Don't be overly polite and let them walk ahead of you. You've worked to become the leader, so lead. Once you get to the appropriate area, you can show them the models, utilizing a technique covered in the next chapter, "Feature-Function-Benefit Selling."

But wait! What if they ask questions? Answer them all positively. If you don't know the answer, say, "I don't know but I will find out." If you have even one answer proven wrong, you'll lose all the credibility you worked so hard to achieve. Don't say no in answer to any of their questions. Say, "Here is what I can do." Never say, "I can't do that."

The charts below illustrate two types of reasoning, or the logic that most people use in drawing conclusions, and demonstrate why my Sales Whisperer™ approach is so comfortable and effective for the salespeople I have trained.

40

Deductive Reasoning

Deductive reasoning is drawing a conclusion based on the acceptance of two premises. If Premise 1 and Premise 2 are each true, then any conclusion based on Premises 1 and 2 must also be true. (This is similar to the logic used in geometric proofs. If A=B and B=C, then logic dictates that A=C.)

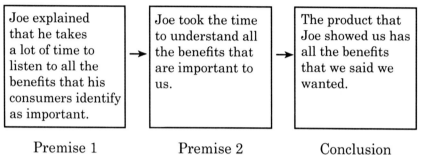

Premise 1   Premise 2   Conclusion

Inductive Reasoning

When we draw a conclusion that is reasonable and probably true, based on specific, observable events, we are employing inductive reasoning. Unlike deductive reasoning, inductive reasoning is not clear proof, yet it allows us to form hypotheses and theories that we can then test.

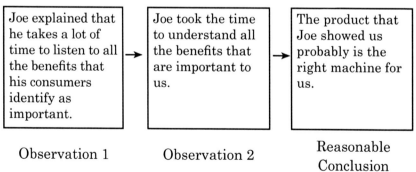

Observation 1   Observation 2   Reasonable Conclusion

(Charts adapted from Wade and Tavris 2003, 316-17)

Whether a consumer applies deductive or inductive reasoning, when you explain that you take a lot of time to listen to all the benefits that your consumers identify as important, and then take the time to understand all the benefits that are important to your consumers, they will reach the logical (and true) conclusion that the product you showed them will meet all their needs.

When practicing the Sales Whisperer™ method, remember to:

- Ask the (proper) questions that will uncover the bottom-line benefit for each specific consumer (remember my mistakes).

- Never presume. Always assume that each consumer's needs are unique, and that each consumer's needs are different.

- Listen twice as much as you talk.

- Ask follow-up questions until you're certain you understand the consumer's bottom-line needs.

- Write the bottom-line needs down. It won't intimidate them; rather, they'll appreciate and respect your attention to their needs.

- Say, "Follow me," then LEAD the consumer to the item or product that will fulfill all the needs that they identified.

Chapter 6

Feature – Function – Benefit Selling

As I hope you've learned by now, nobody invests a large amount of money for features. They need, in fact, to understand how they function and the only thing they actually buy is the benefit they'll derive from owning what you're selling. From what I've seen, most salespeople feature the consumer to death and hardly spend any time on the benefits. Sell the benefits! There's a pot of gold awaiting you when you sell the benefits—I promise!

As I pointed out before, salespeople have the experience that consumers or buyers lack when they enter your world. Consumers expect you to have this expertise, and hope that you'll share it with them in a professional and helpful way. Let consumers and buyers know that you do indeed have experience and will share it with them.

If done correctly, you can get them in the calm, submissive state you worked so hard to achieve when you prepared this morning; when you reminded yourself of the different ways that men and women learn; and when you greeted your consumers or buyers. You maintained their calm, submissive state by asking questions professionally. You stated their purpose in order to identify the true bottom-line benefits you need to know in order to assist them in making an intelligent buying decision. In doing so, you created the perception that the benefits they told you they wanted are indeed the ONLY remedies for their problem. Now you're ready to continue this mindset with the Feature-Function-Benefit selling technique.

First, state the feature properly. Don't use nicknames for the feature. Manufacturers spend a lot of money researching names that will be well received by consumers. When you call it by another name, or call it "this gadget, this thing, or this widget," you dilute the intended impact on the consumer. If it's apparent that you don't know the proper name or title for a product or feature, it also dilutes your professionalism in the consumers' eyes. Would you invest $3,000 on a product with a salesperson—someone you're depending upon to help guide you to the most prudent way to spend your money—if he or she didn't even know the proper name of a feature? Salespeople lose credibility—and control—at this point. Now you have to jump a hurdle that you created. A hurdle that didn't have to be there.

After you properly state the feature, it's time to explain the functionality. It's as if you're saying, "This is what it's called, and here is how it works." Being able to articulate how a feature works increases your professionalism and credibility with consumers. It reassures them when they know that, with your experienced guidance, they'll have all of the pertinent facts and will be able to make a rational and correct decision.

I know we've all had clients or consumers who once read a *Popular Mechanics* magazine while waiting in a dentist's office and feel that that makes them qualified to build a car! They want to know every little thing about everything, and sometimes try to trip you up so they can display their immense knowledge of electronics, physics, and mechanics acquired from a three-page article they read years ago. Defer to their ego because you're trying to make a sale. Fortunately, this doesn't happen often, but when it does, it's important that you have at least a general knowledge of how a feature works. Most people will accept your short description and be ready to move on. The important thing is to maintain the rhythm of the sales presentation.

Notice that I said sales presentation. I'm sure that you

have heard—many times, as I have—this referred to as a sales pitch. A circus barker pitches. Someone at a flea market booth pitches. Sales Whisperers™ do not pitch. They present a quality product. This is the mindset you must have and exemplify. Any other attitude degrades the brand image you want to plant in the consumer's mind. If you allow the image to degrade, you might as well be selling a commodity.

When you sell a commodity, you change the proposition with your consumer or buyer. Instead of giving them a compelling reason BEYOND price to purchase your product, their purchase is dependent ON price. You then have no control of the sale and the possibility of your losing it increases. The product you represent must rise above commodity status in your consumers' eyes. It is YOUR responsibility to make that happen. If you don't address what you're selling with dignity, your target consumers or clients won't.

After you state and properly describe the feature, you then SELL the BENEFITS. We addressed this earlier. Remember, the only thing you sell are the benefits, and you only sell the benefits that you got from the consumer during your fact-finding or discovery period, when you asked qualifying questions as described in Chapter 5. That's when you drilled down to uncover the bottom-line, individualized benefits that are unique to this particular person or persons.

Concentrate only on the benefits that you know are the most important to THIS consumer. Any other benefits afforded by this product or service should be secondary, or even incidental. In other words, all the other available benefits that you might describe to other consumers are no more than NICE to know for this consumer. Focus on what this consumer NEEDS to know in order to make an informed purchase decision.

The easiest way I know of to remember to talk about the benefits with consumers, clients, or buyers is to imagine that they have big red letters saying "So what?" painted on their foreheads. This reminds me to use the transitional phrase,

"So that..." each time I finish explaining a feature and its function. For example, "Here is a feature, and this is how it functions, SO THAT you get the benefit that you said was important when you familiarized me with your dilemma."

When you do this, you're practicing the Sales Whisperer™ technique for maintaining control over the selling situation. Sometimes during this Feature-Function-Benefit (FFB) presentation (not pitch), you may find that you failed to understand the importance of a particular benefit. Do not let your disappointment show. It's normal to miss something occasionally, particularly if you're in a busy setting with other conversations going on nearby. If you do miss a benefit, simply look concerned and say, "With all this going on around us, I must have missed that."

Don't let the consumer draw you into an argument or adversarial position. You could say, "Well you said..." Or, "You didn't say..." but that would be sales suicide. ALWAYS put the blame for a miscommunication on yourself and offer a reason for your mistake. At no time in the selling situation, particularly this late in the game, do you want to win the small battle that will eventually cost you the sale.

Follow your positive statement with, "So that I'm that sure I understand you properly, what would you say IS the most important benefit to you?" Then talk about a feature and function that will provide them with that benefit.

Sales Whisperer™ Tip #1

It is far better—and easier—to unveil something new and different at the FFB part of the presentation than when it's later brought up as an objection. This is especially true when something comes up—and you know eventually it will come up— as something the consumer thinks is a valid argument because they feel the price you're asking is too high. We will discuss this more in the next chapter, "Handling Consumer Objections."

When a consumer doesn't have the patience to save an objection or question until you ask for the order but surprises you with it during the FFB period, it's what we call in the industry a push back. The average clients or consumers may feel that they must always negotiate because they have been programmed to do so by weaker salespeople. When price is the compelling reason for purchase, the odds of a salesperson winning on a consistent basis using that approach are slim. When the consumers balk at the price, those salespeople have to cut the price or risk losing the sale. They cause the problem and then blame the consumer. They never blame themselves for a situation that they brought upon themselves, and they'll never be big-time performers or the true professional that you're attempting to be by purchasing and studying this book.

Sales Whisperer™ Tip #2

Another easy way to remember to always talk about and sell the benefits is to remember that the consumer is thinking, "What's in it for me?" If you imagine this stamped on the forehead of every one of your clients, consumers, or buyers, you'll always remember to sell the benefits.

When you have determined six or seven bottom-line benefits germane to a particular consumer, you must prioritize them. Put them in rank order in your mind as you point out the features and functions that will give consumers the benefits they told you were important to them. Time is very precious to all of us, whether we're a retail consumer, a client buying a house, or a buyer with many appointments each day.

By prioritizing the benefits of the six or seven special ones you pulled out of them, you make sure that you command (not demand) their attention. And even if they run out of patience, you can be sure that you took your best shot at satisfying their top benefit needs. If time seems to be of the essence to them, and you've delivered the very best of their top benefits, maybe it's time for a trial close. What do you think?

If you said yes, then please go to the head of the Sales

Whisperer™ class because I'm proud of you. Now, it's critical to remember that every time you sell a benefit, you should demonstrate it, if possible. Do this even if you don't have the product in front of you, but must paint a mental picture for the consumers.

Sales Whisperer™ Tip #3

PRESENTATION WITHOUT DEMONSTRATION IS JUST CONVERSATION. I don't know who originally said this, but I first remember hearing it 25 years ago. The better salespeople have been saying it for a long time. You must cultivate and increase the visual learner's interest (most women) through demonstration while describing benefits for the auditory learner (most men). Not only does this cover both visual and auditory learners, it provides your consumers with a redundancy of information, and that's the best way to ensure that learning occurs.

Sales Whisperer™ Tip #4

Get the consumer physically involved.

It's critical during FFB to get consumers involved when you demonstrate features in order to sell the benefit. When you do this, however, you should always stay in what I call the Power Position. For example, if you demonstrate the amount of legroom in the back seat of a car, have the consumers get in and sit down while you remain standing, so that they have to look up at you. If you're selling a refrigerator, and say how easy it is to remove the bottom crisper for cleaning, have the consumers squat down to try it. They get to feel the product and see how easy it is, and, again, they have to look up at you when you speak. This sends them another subliminal message that you are in charge.

This does NOT feel like pressure. It's comforting; they feel that they're in contact with an expert who will help them. You don't actually say this aloud, but it is indeed the message most people will receive. This strengthens your position of power.

Have you ever noticed that when you purchased a big-ticket item like an automobile, most of the serious negotiations for price and options took place inside the salesperson's office? Did you notice that you were sitting down? There's a good possibility that the salesperson's chair was slightly taller than the one in which you sat. Do you suppose he or she was sending you a subliminal message? I guarantee that you'll be looking for things like this in future negotiations, and if you do, think of me smiling somewhere, would you please?

If you watch your consumers closely, you'll detect buying signs.

Body Language:

- If you're both sitting down, is the consumer sitting on the edge of his or her seat? If so, it's time for a trial close.

- Slumping in the chair? You've miscalculated the importance of the benefit you're selling. Quickly finish what you're saying and switch gears, smoothly, to another bottom-line benefit.

- Are their eyes fixed on you? Are they intent on what you're saying? If you're on your last benefit, finish and close the deal. If not, finish and go to the next benefit.

Verbal signs:

- If they have a constant smile, close the deal.

- If they ask about financing, explain it and close the deal.

- If they look at their checkbook, close the deal.

- If a consumer asks what his or her spouse thinks and the spouse responds positively, close the deal.

Attention retention:

Is it apparent that they understand and agree with what you say? Write the order.

These are some of the buying signals I describe and demonstrate in my seminars. The attendees quickly become Sales Whisperers™ with critical eyes. If you follow the program and apply the knowledge and techniques you learned in the first few chapters, you'll be a Sales Whisperer™ too.

If you are successful during the FFB segment, many times the consumers will close the deal themselves and that's the end of it. You simply need to write the order or ask for the P.O.

Watch for buying signs the whole way through your presentation. After you've guided consumers into a calm, submissive state and discovered all their bottom-line benefits; after you have properly stated the features; briefly described the functions; and then sold the benefits that they admitted they needed, there is a good chance there will be no objections and you will not have to use a closing technique.

After you explain the final benefit and have them confirm that all their needs have been met, write the order. The sale is done.

Chapter 7

Handling Consumer Objections

Up to this point, you've spent a lot of time and effort to get and keep your consumer or buyer in a calm, submissive state. This is NOT the time to lose control. You have way too much invested in this sale to let it slip away now. Keep your cool even (and especially) if the client with which you're working does not.

When consumers object to or balk at something, what are they really saying? No. They just said no to you by expressing doubt. When a buyer, client, or consumer says NO, what do they really mean? When they say NO, they actually mean KNOW!

In the informal surveys I have conducted over the years with some of the best salespeople in the United States, I have found that this is actually the case. My personal experience, as well as that of other top salespeople, leads me to believe that when the consumer says NO, approximately three out of four times they're not saying no to you personally, so please don't make the mistake of taking it that way. Nor are they expressing a dislike of the product you're presenting. What they're saying is that they need to KNOW more about it before they make a purchase decision.

This may mean that you're guilty of not doing a good enough job of revealing the consumers' real bottom-line benefits. You may also have neglected to confirm that their benefit needs were in fact addressed and satisfied. What this tells me is that approximately three out of four times, salespeople are at fault for creating this situation, so don't blame the consumer. Look in the mirror. It isn't always our fault but I hope you've noticed a common theme so far in the Sales Whisperer™ psychology. It's imperative that you take the time to ask as many questions as you need to harvest the major bottom-line benefits that are important to and will excite the consumer. The better you are in this questioning period, the easier the sale will be. The longer you take asking the right discovery or fact-finding questions, the less time the presentation of a quality product will take and the higher the probability you will be able skip the objection stage and get right to closing the sale.

You'll be amazed that even with the longer questioning period, your total time to make the sale will be about the same as or less than you're used to experiencing. The major difference you'll see is that you're ringing the cash register much more often than before. On this point, please let me assure you. If you don't believe me yet, trust me for now.

When an objection is raised, once again keep your cool. Maintain that even keel we talked about before. The uninformed salesperson will try to act superior and say, "I've never heard a person say that before!" Of course, they're trying a little reverse psychology. If a salesperson said that to you following an objection or question you raised, how would you feel? Most people will feel anger. The uninformed salesperson might as well have said, "Nobody else has ever made that stupid comment or assertion to me before!"

Bingo! You have put yet another hurdle between yourself and your client—and yourself and your sale. The consumers feel that they have just been belittled by the salesperson. I would not spend my money with someone who belittled me. Neither would you and neither will your consumer unless you get REALLY lucky. The salesperson, who is more of a clerk or order taker at this point, is certainly not exercising the skill set of a seasoned professional. Now he or she has transformed the consumer's calm, submissive emotional state to an adversarial one.

The salesperson is no longer enjoying a collaborative relationship with the buyer or consumer. At best, this puts the salesperson (clerk) back at square one. At worst, the consumer gives up, leaves, and heads for that proverbial "one more place" that consumers always talk about.

Sales Whisperer™ Tip #5

I don't believe in "Be-backs." When consumers leave, most of the time they don't come back.

If I ever go back in the retail business, I might name my store One More Place, simply because that's where most of the consumers who did not buy from me said they were headed. They would say, "Well this is the first place I stopped. I've got one more place to go." At that point I could say "Lady (or mister), you're already there," while I pointed to the sign on my building!

When consumers say, "I've got one more place to check, an uninformed salesperson would probably say, "Here's my card. Ask for me when you come back." Ever notice all the business cards in the parking lot when you leave to go home at night? I rest my case.

When you're challenged by an objection, react in a calm manner.

I'll say it again and again.

The first thing you need to do is keep your cool. Then you need to implement what I call the Cushioning Technique. It starts with a transitional phrase like the examples below.

"I understand how you feel."

Now, there's a statement that would not make anyone angry, nor would it embarrass anyone. You're just being consistent with what you've been doing since the consumer walked in your door.

"If I were in your shoes I'd feel the same way."

Here you continue to show empathy for the consumer or client. Again, this is consistent with what you've been doing since the consumer walked in the door.

"You're not my first consumer to bring that up."

Clearly, this is much better than saying, "I've never heard THAT before!" I know you've heard people say this, and it just doesn't work. At that point, you would be building a fence between you and the consumer.

"I'm not surprised to hear you ask that question."

This puts the consumer at ease, for as we discussed earlier, there is safety in numbers for many people. Thinking that others have asked this question, the consumer stays calm and submissive—just where you want to keep them.

"I congratulate you on having done your research."

A compliment is absolutely not what the average consumer expects to hear. Their tenseness dissipates.

"I can tell you put a lot of thought into that."

Wow! Do you think this statement would make the client or buyer angry? Of course not.

"I agree this is important to you based on what you said before."

This keeps THE consumer as YOUR consumer and NOT a problem.

"I can tell that this is really troubling you."

Then say, "I probably did not explain it properly. Let me rectify that."

Sales Whisperer™ Tip #6

Always put the blame on yourself. You can smile later, after you figure out how much commission you just made by swallowing your pride.

See anything here that would turn the consumer or buyer off? I would think not. I haven't had anybody feel pressured or uneasy with any of these cushioning replies. I have had, however, tons of people who felt very much at ease after hearing one of these, as opposed to the way they felt when they were anticipating voicing an objection or question. The relief they feel after that build-up not only keeps them in that calm, submissive state, it almost puts them to sleep they're so relaxed.

The important thing to remember here is that there are many cushioning phrases that work beautifully. After reading the examples above, I'm sure you can think of many more. The key is to have a number of them at your disposal and review them from time to time. You need to have them roll off your tongue very easily on your command.

What if the consumer or buyer has more than one question or objection? You'd look and feel kind of silly saying, "I understand how your feel." Then the consumer voices another objection and you say, "I understand how you feel." Maybe they have another objection and you say, "I understand how you feel."

This cannot continue. You need to stockpile at least four cushioning statements that are easy for you to remember. If you have them at your disposal, you should NEVER fear an objection.

While I'm thinking about it, novice salespeople fear handling objections more than anything else, and I often wonder why. This morning, running errands, I saw a construction project and some workers walking a plank about five stories high. I remember thinking that I was glad I didn't have to do THAT for a living. And you know, I have never read a magazine or newspaper headline saying,

"Salesperson killed asking for the order!" Nor have I heard anything about a salesperson that was killed by a consumer's objection. We're actually in a very safe profession.

All right, let's get back to this objection business. After you properly cushion the objection (it's so easy and fun to do and so effective that it should be illegal), it's time to add a transitional phrase. Let's say your cushioning statement was, "I understand how you feel." Your next phrase might be, "Some of my other consumers have expressed the same question or concern." Here again, there is nothing in your statement to make the consumers feel uncomfortable. You've reminded them that you've had other consumers who raised a similar concern. They're again relieved.

Wait! What did I just say? Some of my other WHAT expressed that same concern? Some of my other C-O-N-S-U-M-E-R-S! Notice the subliminal message in that statement. If they were my CONSUMERS, they must have ended up buying from me—even though they expressed a similar concern! I guarantee that most consumers will notice this and will be anxious to hear what you say next. It must be something that made sense to all their fellow consumers.

Now you hit them with the trump phrase: "I understand how you FEEL. Some of my other consumers have FELT the same way..." (Here it comes...) "Until they FOUND..." Kaboom!

Until they found...what? Consumers will be trying to keep their composure as you reach a crescendo in your friendly but astute response. (Fun, isn't it? If you think it's fun to read, wait until you add this to your arsenal, and can watch the consumers' faces for real!) Have you noticed that I have never actually addressed the objection? This particular technique takes just five seconds to say. Then, and ONLY then are you ready to address the question or objection.

If you're selling a house, one concern might be that the buyers' monthly payments will be $100 more a month than they were prepared to pay. You say (you all know this by heart now, right?), "I understand how you feel. An extra $100 a month is a lot of money for me too."

"Some of my other consumers have expressed that same concern. In this case, however, did you notice that the new furnace, air conditioner, and many of the kitchen appliances are Energy Star-rated, and that the estimated year-round projected dollar savings on this house is approximately $80 a month compared to the other houses we went through?

"This means that, overall, you really are only paying an additional $20 per month to get the house that offers you ALL the benefits that you said were important to you—and more! $20 per month is only $5 a week or $.71 per day difference. I know people who spend over $5 per day on cigarettes. I understood before I showed you this house that it would require more of a monthly payment than you told me you wanted, but when I learned about the energy savings I knew you would recognize the value."

Ha! Tell me the consumer that would turn that down. Most of them would understand and agree with your rationalization. After the cushioning kept the consumer on the same page, you helped them RATIONALIZE the value of this house. That's what pros can and should do. The Sales Whisperer™ program helps you do just that—and have fun doing it.

The important thing to remember is that you may think you're helping the consumer to rationalize why they're spending more money than they anticipated, or getting a completely different model than they thought they wanted, and you would be right. They may need you to help them rationalize, not only to themselves, but also to people who will be surprised that they paid so much.

Sales Whisperer™ Tip #7

Always be able to give your consumer the "Yeah, buts" for which they're looking!

When a neighbor, spouse, or other family member says, "You spent way more than you said you would," the consumer needs to be able to say:

"Yeah, but this model will last longer, which partially offsets the variance in price."

"Yeah, but this is an Energy Star model that will save me X dollars each year in energy costs."

"Yeah, but it has all the benefits I wanted and more."

"Yeah, but I got a longer warranty with this."

Who do you think provided them with all these "Yeah, buts"? If consumers pay more than they planned, and get every benefit for which they were looking, and are able to defend their purchase decision using the information they got from the salesperson, then that salesperson must have been a Sales Whisperer™. That professional just might be you when you finish reading this book. I certainly hope so.

Use this technique. Don't deviate from it. If you cushion an objection by saying, "I understand how you feel," and then say, "but…," you've erased virtually everything you said before. All the goodwill you garnered will evaporate when you say, "But." Please take "but" out of your vocabulary.

The whole point of this chapter is to impress upon you that you should not let an objection turn your friendly relationship with this consumer into one that's just about the transaction. Continue to keep it on a collaborative level. After reading this, I think a lot of you will.

There are also objections disguised as questions, what I call stealth objections. You can finesse those too. We touched a little bit on this earlier. For example, "Is this your best price?" The uninformed answer: "I can drop the price $20 if you buy today."

What does this tell you about the salesperson? What does it tell the consumers? Maybe that the salesperson was not forthcoming? That the salesperson tried to cheat you? Would you buy from that person? No and neither will your consumers buy from you if you do that. Instead of dropping the price $20, help consumers rationalize the extra expense.

(Don't forget to cushion first.) "This is a very fair price for the benefits and quality you demand.

"I know that you don't want to settle for less than all the things that are important to you. You know that the average life of this is 15 years, so you'll enjoy it for a long time. That extra $20 is only $1.33 a year, or just less than $.03 a day. You'll save far more than that with the benefit of this feature (whatever it may be) over the price of a lesser model. I'm sure you'll agree it's worth the extra initial $20."

"I'm sure you'll agree" reinforces your message in the consumer's mind.

Things to remember:

- Human nature makes us all ask for more of a discount than we actually and rationally expect to receive.
- Consumers NEVER lie about a competitor's price, or do they?

The Cushioning Technique will control even those consumers who fabricate the truth. In some cases, it may be easier to cushion the objection and then convert it to a question. For example, "I understand how you feel. Is the question (don't say objection)…?" Then restate the concern in the form of a question.

After reinforcing for the consumers that they had a question (not an objection), answer the question. Ask if you've answered the question (not objection). If you receive a positive response, close the sale.

If the answer is no, swallow your ego and say, "I guess I missed something. I'm sorry. What specifically is your question?" Then repeat the process and ask for the order.

This is another example of a psychological set. You're telling consumers, subliminally, that they don't have an objection, only a question. This is all about friendly control and it's fun! It's one of several ways to use friendly persuasion to influence attitudes: repetition of information increases the perception of validity for the listener.

Another way, already discussed in Chapter 1, is what I call Keeping Up with the Jones', in which consumers associate themselves, by virtue of purchasing your product, with an admired or attractive person. Think celebrity endorsements, or commercials featuring sexy men and women. Or think of yourself saying, "A lot of Ford and GM executives live in this neighborhood."

You can also lead consumers to associate your presentation with a good feeling, (such as that experienced by two friends meeting over a meal). For example, "Let's have a cup of coffee and discuss this." (Wade and Tavris 2003, 281)

Sometimes you have to help consumers rationalize their purchase decision in a different way. Some consumers need to consider and weigh opposing facts or ideas before they can make a decision. The technical term for this is dialectical reasoning, but it's what we do when we weigh the pros and cons of an issue or decision. (Wade and Tavris 2003, 318-319) You've probably done this yourself. It can be a powerful sales tool.

It's a simple process, but the more complex the problem, the more helpful a simple list seems to be for people. There are those who can do the same thing in their heads, but others, particularly those who learn by touch, find it's most helpful to write things down before analyzing the issue. Encourage those consumers to make a chart showing the pros and cons. Help them list all the pros you can, but let them come up with the cons on their own. And when they do come up with one, cushion it and convert it to a question. This allows them to rationalize the value of your product or service and to reach a reasonable and logical conclusion.

Sales Whisperer™ Tip #8

Consumers need you to orchestrate a rationalization moment in order to free them to make a purchase decision. Always use a chart when consumers must make a large financial decision and they clearly need to weigh the pros and cons.

Please remember that you are one of the few—or maybe even the only—salesperson who took time to uncover their required bottom-line benefits. You identified their true benefit needs. Your fact-finding questions not only revealed their needs, they helped put you within the consumers' circle of trust. Help them with the positives. Intercede when they have a negative and turn it into a question. Answer the question and it probably will become a positive or at the very least, a neutral.

With the Sales Whisperer™ psychology, you orchestrate the time that consumers need to put pressure on themselves to make a decision. You make sure it's the right decision so they seek you out when it's time to make another purchase and refer you to their family and friends. And that's exactly what you want: referrals and repeat business.

Chapter 8

Closing the Sale

<u>**Sales Whisperer™ Tip #9**</u>
Allow consumers to close the sale themselves.

After you receive the final confirmation that you've satisfied all of the consumer's needed benefits, write the order and ask for delivery address, etc. More times than I'll bet you'd believe, the consumer is just waiting for a little push and this is when you can ORCHESTRATE—not APPLY—pressure.

Having consumers close themselves is the objective of everything I've talked about to this point. The understanding of human psychology and the selling skills all intertwine to control the selling situation. Up to this point you're comfortable with what you do, when you do it, and why you do it. This should get you ready to join the top 20% of salespeople. All you must do is earnestly apply your knowledge.

The Pareto Principle outlines the 80/20 rule. The top 20% of salespeople produce 80% of the total revenue! Pretty revealing, huh? If a salesperson were to rise to the top 20% of the top 20% of all salespeople, he or she would be in the top 4%, earnings-wise, of all salespeople. Those top salespeople are successful because they dedicate themselves to success, and know how to close the sale.

If you expect to find a magic potion in this chapter that guarantees the sale in all situations, you're going to be disappointed. Such a potion simply does not exist and never has. On the other hand, by now you know that the whole idea of the Sales Whisperer™ psychology is to put yourself in a position of leadership by controlling every segment of the selling situation. You no longer fear handling consumer objections (because it's fun and simple), and when you finish this chapter you'll have more closing techniques.

If you do realize all of that, you will truly be of great assistance to your consumers and buyers. And you are probably perceptive and intuitive enough to consider wearing the official Sales Whisperer™ badge (if there were such a thing). If this is the case, get ready to wear it proudly. Now, there may not be an actual badge, but you can certainly make the money a true Sales Whisperer™ makes, and that is what's most important to you is it not? It is to me.

Utilizing psychology and recognizing how different people think and process information has put you in a very powerful but benevolent position, and that very much increases your chances of not having to attempt a close at all.

Still, some people just will not cooperate by closing themselves. Some people, not because of anything you said or did, are reluctant to "get off the dime," and need to be gently nudged for their own good. After all, you've worked very diligently to find out what the true bottom-line benefits are and why they're unique and important to the consumer. You know from that on-the-spot research what will suit them best; make them comfortable with their choice, and happy in their purchase decision many years down the road. You did not SELL them something. Because of your great care and attention to discovering their wants and needs, you can be confident that you made a problem go away for the consumer or client, while supplementing your income at the same time.

At this point, you've invested too much time and effort NOT to close the sale. If you used the psychology from the previous chapters, you're probably the only salesperson who took the time and made the effort to expertly dissect your consumer's or client's problem and uncover the true bottom-line benefits. You deserve the sale.

John Greenleaf Whittier wrote, "For of all sad words of tongue or pen, The saddest are these: 'It might have been!'" That should be the official credo of sales pretenders, not that of true sales professionals. I'm sure you agree. I'm sure you agree—get it? Got you! I just used a psychological set on you! The difference is, it's the truth, and I'm quite confident that you already agree with me. When I said, "I'm sure you agree," I used an assumptive close. I did not ask you if you agreed, I set you up to agree. If you had disagreed, you would have had to defend your position, and most people are not prepared to do that. With an assumptive close you're fostering compliance.

If a close is necessary, here are some things to consider. They'll make your job easier, and keep you in control and doing the right thing for the consumer.

The ABCs of Closing

The best salespeople are always closing. They're always alert to any buying signal that would allow them to consummate the sale. This doesn't necessarily mean they have to pressure the client as if they were in the kill zone (although some do). It really means that they're always seeking the opportunity to close the deal and get on to the next opportunity to sell something.

When you attempt to close, make sure you don't do it in a way that will unnerve consumers or alert them to the fact that you've entered the closing mode. They can read body language just as you can, and if they're focused, they too can detect even subtle deviations in your normal speech or manner. Don't change your posture in any extreme way or a red flag will be raised, alerting consumers to be on guard. Don't change your vocal inflection or your rate of speech, or you risk having the consumers put up defenses.

Consumers can try to stall the sale at any time. If they feel pressured, they might use one of many stalling techniques. For example, the consumer says, "I'm not ready to buy today." You say, "Oh?" And then shut up. Bite your tongue if you must. What seems like an hour will only be seconds. Because of your strategic pause, most consumers will offer what they feel is a good excuse, given the short time that they've had to create one.

Here's one of the most popular excuses: "I have to talk to my wife (or husband)."

Now, how many of you would seriously consider the purchase of a big-ticket item like a plasma TV or a dining room set without at least discussing it with your spouse first? You and I would be in big trouble if we bought something of that nature without the knowledge of our spouses. With that in mind, "I have to talk to my wife (or husband)," seems, on the surface, like a prudent reason to delay a purchase—which is why you should never show disappointment or anger that they wasted your time or toyed with you by raising your expectations of making a sale. On the other hand, since they didn't offer to put some earnest money down, ask you to hold the item or put it in layaway, they may leave and be closed somewhere else. Remember most people who are Be-backs won't be back at all to buy that item from you. They'll shop until another salesperson closes them.

So after you execute the strategic pause and the consumer gives you the "I have to talk to my spouse" excuse, respond with a cushioning statement. For example, "I certainly can understand that. $3,300 is a lot of money to my wife and me too." Then say, "I have to assume you've discussed the possibility of your purchasing this though, right?" The consumer will probably respond in the affirmative, and with a sheepish grin. Instead of letting him or her walk away, or beginning an uncomfortable debate about who wears the pants in the family (eek!), you've showed empathy and asked a reasonable question.

Follow that with another question. "Is there still a question in your mind about this set I have on sale?" If the consumer says yes, ask him or her to share the question, and then answer it. It is then time for another trial close, such as, "You know, I only have two of these sets left and it fits so nicely with what you told me you needed, why don't you put $200 down and I'll hold it for a day or two until you can bring your husband (or wife) in to see it?" Once you get the $200, you've taken a big step towards closing. Consumers will do everything they can to convince their spouse to agree to purchase this item or items because they want to avoid the embarrassment of coming back in to get their $200 back. It's just human nature.

When you ask if they still have any questions about the product and they say, "No," follow up with, "Since you said that you had discussed this with your husband (or wife) before you came in, are there any questions that you feel she (or he) might have that I can answer for you?" Notice that you're not arguing with the consumer. You're only asking the proper questions. Even if they choose not to put money down, make sure that when consumers goes home to talk to their spouse they'll have all the answers to any questions they anticipate their spouse may pose.

If they say, "I've got one more place to look," respond the same way. Cushion and ask questions.

No matter what excuse consumers give, you have to understand that there is some reason they're not buying or putting money down right now, and it could very well be that they're not being forthcoming with their true objection. By cushioning and following up with fact-finding or discovery questions, more often than not (by a wide margin), their objection or concern will surface because your questions have exhausted all their excuses

When that question or concern is finally uncovered, cushion the objection, convert it to a question and re-state it, then ask the consumer to confirm your understanding of the QUESTION (which is no longer an objection because you just transformed it into a question and reinforced that mindset). Answer the question and try another close.

As I pointed out earlier, watch for buying signals and be prepared to close at every opportunity. You never want to risk talking yourself out of the sale, and this happens far too many times to uninformed salespeople. Have I been guilty of this? Of course I have. With practice and intense attention to what consumers say and how they say it, it doesn't happen very often any more. Have you been guilty of this? If you're honest with yourself, the answer would have to be yes as well.

Closing is a cardinal rule in retail, and in wholesale when you feel the consumer can be closed on the spot. The interesting thing is that when you close, most often consumers are relieved that the ordeal is over, and with the psychology we use, they're proud of their decision. Over and above that, they take themselves totally out of the market. A lot of salespeople are concerned that the consumer will see an ad for a lower price somewhere else and then come back the next day and complain. The truth is, people who do that represent a very small percentage of the whole.

Most people are so relieved that the purchase decision has been consummated that they no longer notice anything to do with furniture (or whatever your product or concept is). They could buy a loveseat from you, look at the paper that night, see a competitive furniture store's ad, and in most cases, look dead square at it—and not even notice the price of loveseats. They'll treat the ad as throwaway material. They're out of the market, and glad to be in that position.

For longer-term sales, such as real estate, it's next to impossible to get buyers to offer a contract on the first house you show them. Be aware of the situation and use common sense on when to orchestrate the consumers' ability to put pressure on themselves.

The absolute best time to close or at least execute a trial close is when you recognize a buying sign. A few examples of buying signs follow. The prospect:

- noticeably speeds up the pace of his or her speech or acts excited to move ahead.

- noticeably slows down the pace, appearing not to be keeping up with the sales presentation. This very often means that he or she is doing a mental analysis. (Can I afford this? Will my wife like this? What will my husband say when I tell him I spent this much?) It might also mean he or she is rationalizing the decision. It's time to ask for the order.

- starts peppering you with excited questions. It's time to close.

- asks questions about the terms of the purchase (such as cash discount, credit cards accepted, available financing). Answer the question and write the order. If consumers ask these questions early in your presentation, they're not ready to buy yet. These are "safety zone" questions. They represent things consumers would like to think about while you're showing them the product, and they know that's a safe time to ask.

- asks how long it will take to get the item. You could give them an answer, but to retain control, ask them a question back. "How soon do you need it?" Two "control elements" happen here: first, whatever answer you eventually give makes them feel that they're in control and that you're accommodating them; second, you discover when they want it delivered, and sometimes why. In other words, you can judge their sense of urgency. If the date that they need it is close, you know that the odds are extremely high that they're buying TODAY from SOMEBODY. Make sure that somebody is you.

Now, let's examine some extremely effective closes.

Urgency Close

"The sale ends today." While not original, it is sometimes effective when used on the right people. If you've been observant, you'll have a fairly firm understanding of your consumers and their tolerance for this kind of close. Let's face it, sometimes the sale DOES end today, and this is a technique that should be used when it's the truth. Take advantage of the same technique if the sale ends Saturday. Any time there is a legitimate timeline that ends in the near future, the urgency close can be and often is an effective tool.

The bargain doesn't have to apply only to the dollar savings, as I'm sure you realize. You can apply it to other favorable offers, such as free consumer financing for a given period of time, free delivery, free installation, and other important items. In real estate sales, it could be a free homeowners warranty, offered for a limited time. You could also offer a discount for a quick sale. Remind consumers that somebody will jump on the deal soon if they don't.

Trial Close

Only when you feel you're on the brink of a close should you ask a question that can be answered with either a yes or a no. NEVER, during the questioning or feature-function-benefit phases should you ask a question that can be answered with a no. This is something I have brought up many times in prior chapters. IF YOU EXECUTE A CLOSING TECHNIQUE AND THE CONSUMER BUYS, THAT'S A CLOSE. IF THE CONSUMER BALKS, THAT'S A TRIAL CLOSE THAT DIDN'T WORK.

If the consumer's answer is negative, you need to find out why. Cushion, restate the objection as a question, and answer the question. After you confirm that you have answered the question, it may be time to try another close. Most trial closes ask a yes/no question, but some are designed to see just how close you are to closing the deal. If that's your intention, make statements or ask open-ended questions such as the ones below.

- "I'll bet this fits the bill for you."
- "I'm sure you recognize why this is such a value."
- "Which of these two models do you like better?"
- "What do you think about getting the extended warranty with this model?"
- "This looks like the model that will solve your problem. Do you need additional information about it?"

If the answer to that last question is no, write the order. If the answer is yes, return to fact-finding questions, answer the questions, and try another close.

Secondary Close

- "Like most people, I'm sure you want the homeowner's warranty with this."
- "Do you want XM radio installed in your new car since we have a special on it?"

Both questions ask the consumer the easy question. It's easier for them to respond in a positive manner to something at a lower dollar cost than to the bigger item they're considering. Once the consumer is over that hump, consider the bigger item sold and start writing the order.

Authorization Close

Don't say, "Sign here." It intimidates some people. Instead, say something like, "This authorizes me to represent you in the selling of your home." Or, "This authorizes me to make this bid on your behalf."

Summary Close

You can orchestrate the consumer to lead you to the place you want to be by using another psychological set. You simply get the consumer or client in the habit of answering yes to all of your questions or comments. By this point, you know all the bottom-line benefits that are important to your consumer. Itemize and present them as questions.

- "This feature gives you this important benefit, correct?"
- "It affords you the most important thing you wanted, right?"
- "Isn't this the benefit you said you had not considered but would love to have?"
- "You really liked this feature when we talked about it, didn't you?

- "You said this would be good for your young daughter and son, right?"
- "Isn't this the only model that offers you this important benefit?"
- "In fact, isn't this the only model that gives you all the benefits YOU TOLD ME (not what I perceived) you need?"
- "You said the sale price fits within your budget, right?"
- "You were surprised by the 0% financing deal, weren't you?"
- "Why don't we set up delivery for Friday so you can start enjoying all the benefits YOU TOLD ME you needed?"

At the very least, because consumers have been programmed to say yes via this Summary Close technique, it will be more difficult for them to say no. If they do say no, however, keep your composure and ask if there was a benefit you missed that they feel this product doesn't offer. If they say yes, cushion and then show them how the product does indeed give them what they mentioned. If they say no, try another closing question that begs the answer yes. For example, "Won't it be a relief to you to solve your problem by Friday?"

When the consumer says yes, write the order. Remember, you're not hoodwinking or cheating consumers. You didn't betray their trust. You listened when they talked. You identified the benefits that were important to them to make their lives easier. Odds are, you are the only salesperson who actually took a great deal of time—during the questioning period—to familiarize yourself with their wants and needs. You're selling the product at a fair price and they'll enjoy this model for years. All you're doing is helping them make a decision.

You're entitled to be paid for your time and effort, and that can only happen if you close the sale. Remember, if you don't close the sale, odds are they're going to buy somewhere from someone else, and then that other salesperson gets the commission. You cannot let that happen. You treated the consumers fairly and with great empathy. You deserve the sale. Don't YOU be afraid to ask for the order.

Assumptive Close

- "I assume you want to take advantage of the free delivery and installation." If the answer is yes, write the order.
- "I guess it's safe to assume that you're happy you got every benefit you wanted on a model that's on sale." If the answer is yes, write the order.
- "It's obvious to me that your husband/wife would appreciate these benefits too." If you get a positive response, write the order.

Choice Close

If you give a consumer a choice you don't give them an opportunity to say no. The Choice Close is sometimes referred to as Alternative Close. They work exactly the same way. If the consumer's answer to any of the following questions (or ones like them) is positive, write the order.

- "Do you want this in white or the almond color?"
- "We can probably close on this property on March 27th or 28th. Which works best for you?"
- "Is Thursday or Friday better for you to receive delivery?"
- "Will you pay by check or credit card?" (Does anyone pay cash anymore?)

Direct Close

- "We solved your problem. I'll ring this up."
- "I can deliver this tomorrow if you give me the go-ahead now."

- "I'm sure you want the service policy with this since it relates to an insurance policy that ends up costing you only $0.20 per day."

When using a direct close it's important to remember that if the direct approach is warranted with that particular client, consumer, or buyer, you need to use it as a last resort. It's the least positive way to ask for the order and the technique most likely to move the subject further away from that proverbial three feet from the sale. It's really the only approach that we have talked about that heightens the possibility for the subject to say no. Sometimes, as I'm sure you're aware, it's the only avenue left to you. Please try to exhaust all the other closing strategies first, though, as they're safer and more consumer-friendly.

Sales Whisperer™ Tip #10

When using a direct close, once you make the statement or ask the question, SHUT UP!

What may seem like an eternity takes only seconds, and here is the important part: the first person who speaks after you use a direct closing method will generally acquiesce. If you speak before they answer you, out of nervousness or in an attempt to add a valid point, you've failed. The big wind you hear at that point is them exhaling with relief because you just let them off the hook. Save your "next valid point" for later if you need it. Once you (for lack of a better word) "challenge" the consumer with a direct close approach, you simply cannot let them off the hook. Why lay down the gauntlet with clients, and then rescue them from having to answer your closing question?

Add-On Sales

Don't forget about supplementing your income by taking advantage of the opportunity to add peripheral sales to the original sale. Notice how I phrased the service policy example in the direct close section above? I actually could have used that phrase in the assumptive close portion as well. We'll talk more about that in Chapter 9: "Bundling or Packaging Options."

Sales Whisperer™ Tip #11

Sell service policies! You get extra commission, the consumer is protected, and your company enhances its gross margin dollar earnings. You know now that most consumers really want them—they just need help rationalizing why.

After the money has exchanged hands, the new owner enjoys peace of mind, knowing that if something happens after the normal manufacturer's warranty has run out, they have a policy that will save them a great deal of money. They're protecting their investment. Surveys conducted after the sale reveal that almost 90% of consumers were very comfortable in their decision to add the extra "insurance," if you will, to their purchase. This 90% statistic surprises most of the salespeople I talk to because they have the perception that consumers believe that the service policy or extended warranty is just an extra profit-maker for the seller. It does in fact add to the gross revenue and profit margin of the seller; however, just one major service call can totally offset the cost of the warranty for the life of the product. It really is a good deal for consumers, and they'll be happy to have it.

There are two ways to help you make more commission by selling extended warranties and service policies. First, you can do the math and help your consumer rationalize how little it costs them per day (reference the $0.20 per day I used above). Secondly, you can say with confidence that, "About 90% of my consumers are very pleased with the service policy and are very happy they added it." Here you're using the "safety in numbers" or "decisions by association" assurance that I addressed earlier.

The bottom line is don't be afraid to sell the service policies. I say again, it helps your company's margin of profit, strengthening its financial condition, and adds to your commission. Those are both good things. And once they have them, consumers appreciate them. Remember that you can soften the impact in the consumers' minds by using your Sales Whisperer™ skills to help them rationalize how affordable service policies are and how much sense they make. You should sell them with great confidence, because they really are a good thing for everyone concerned.

Keep It Sold

Remember to congratulate your consumers or buyers for making a wise choice based on the benefits they told you they wanted. This reaffirms that they were correct in their decision and helps to prevent buyer's remorse.

Tell consumers that you'll call them after the delivery to make sure everything went as you promised. This normally cements the sale, because you're now like an insurance policy to them. They know you'll follow up on the sale. There will be more information on this in Chapter 10: "After-Sale Selling."

For those of you who are visual learners, I've included a flow chart outlining the selling skills I discussed in the last few chapters.

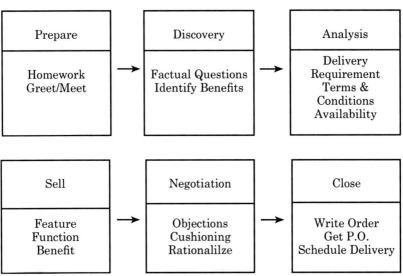

Prepare	Discovery	Analysis
Homework Greet/Meet	Factual Questions Identify Benefits	Delivery Requirement Terms & Conditions Availability

Sell	Negotiation	Close
Feature Function Benefit	Objections Cushioning Rationalilze	Write Order Get P.O. Schedule Delivery

Chapter 9

Bundling or Packaging Opportunities

There is real opportunity to make additional sales after you've earned enough of your consumers' trust for them to commit to a purchase from you. Now is the time to attempt to "package" or "bundle" other items with the item they've already purchased. It's like piggybacking on the larger sale.

It doesn't matter what you're selling. You could be selling tangible items, such as houses, cars, furniture, TVs, major appliances, or intangible items such as health or life insurance. While nobody can possibly close all consumers on these additional purchases, a surprising number will at least listen receptively. You'll be surprised at the percentage that will actually add something—again, because they trust you, and because you help them rationalize the additional purchase.

Every additional item that you add to the original purchase is purely incremental income for you. Keep track of your incremental sales for one year and I guarantee you'll be a believer. You'll be able to quantify your additional earnings and see how much more you made in sales, profits, and commission. Like anything else in sales, you have to track everything you do in order to appreciate what your starting point was and how successful you have been. My experience suggests that if you use the same psychology you used in your original selling experience, you could realize upwards of 20% in incremental sales without having one more consumer than usual. If we cut that in half and say that, in a given year, you only close an incremental sale for 10% of your consumers. Do the math and you'll be amazed at the difference in your annual income.

As with the original selling experience, when selling peripherals you need to help your consumer (or buyer) distinguish between wants and needs. Help them to recognize and acknowledge the benefits of adding what you suggest. They'll be able to get everything they desire, and everything they're able to afford. It doesn't make sense to let them decide later that they need something that would have made sense at the time of sale—had you thought to explain it. Because they WILL end up buying it somewhere else. Some other salesperson will enjoy the sale that should have been yours.

Let's examine a few scenarios.

A consumer purchases a big screen TV and finances $3000. The monthly payment, based on 18% interest for a three-year period, is $108.46. Adding a $250 top-of-the-line DVD player, which you know they'll enjoy for years, only increases their monthly payment to $117.50. The variance is only $9.04 per month more, or only an additional $2.26 per week. But, in fact, the figure you should use is that it's only $.30 more a day! The DVD will be used a lot, and many people spend more than $.30 per day on gum.

You sell consumers an automobile for X amount down and they finance $20,000 over a 5-year period at a 4% interest rate. Their monthly payment would be $368.33. You say that with their two small children, they'll thank you later if they upgrade to leather seats because they're so much easier to clean, and wear so much better than any fabric. You explain that it's on special and only an $850 upgrade, which raises their monthly payment by only $15.65 per month, $3.91 per week, or just $.52 a day. They'll probably use this car every day. What a bargain $.52 a day is, to take away all their concerns about the kids spilling different substances on those seats over the next five years. You might say, "Think how much easier it would be to clean leather seats (and you KNOW you'll have to clean them) versus fabric seats." You promote the ease of cleaning for $.52 a day, and they get the luxuriousness of leather and the higher resale value of the car, for no extra cost. What else do people pay $.52 per day on that would be more important than this?

You sell a new home and your client agrees to finance $200,000 over 30 years at a 6% interest rate. They're not escrowing taxes in their payment. The monthly payment would be $1199.10. You have the ability to sell them an automatic sprinkler system, installed before they move in, for only $2000. This means they may never again have to waste their time standing out in the yard watering the lawn. It also means that they never have to worry about neglecting the time-consuming (and boring) duty of watering their lawn. Because you took the time to ask the right questions and learned about their lifestyle, you can suggest something else, something better, that they would enjoy doing with their time. They can get this great enhancement for only $11.99 per month more. After agreeing to monthly payments of $1199.10, what's another $11.99 per month to get this wonderful convenience? I'll tell you: It's only $3.00 more per week or $.40 per day. Depending on the climate, they might have to water the lawn nearly every day (which is how often it should be done) and with a sprinkler system, they could do it AUTOMATICALLY. So they can play golf or tennis, spend more time with the kids, or do whatever they want to do.

You sell a sofa to a consumer for $1,800. She wants to finance $1500 for 5 years. The interest rate is 18%. Her monthly payment would be $38.09. You know that you have two end tables, for $175 each, which would go beautifully with the sofa. Together, they would just take over a room. The difference to your consumer would be a mere $8.89 more per month, which amounts to $2.23 per week or only

$.30 per day more. You might, as a feeling-finding question, say, "Maggie, how would you feel if I told you I could make you a deal that would really make your day?" What's she going to say, "No, I don't want a deal"? You say, "I'm going to let you have both of these end tables that you've been admiring to go with the new sofa and (insert a strategic pause here)...it will only cost you $.30 per day more! I know you agree that's a bargain." When she agrees that it's a bargain, add it to the sales ticket. Remember, she'll see the sofa and end tables every day. She'll enjoy the them every day, and all for a mere $.30 a day. She got a wonderful deal, and you just made commission on another $350.

I'm sure you're getting the picture. This technique is easy and fun to do. Your consumers will be happier and much more loyal because you pointed out a real bargain. And you (significant pause)... WILL MAKE MORE MONEY.

Sales Whisperer™ Tip #12

You can use this rationalization for selling service policies or anything else you can imagine. If you can imagine it, it can be sold by bundling or packaging it with any larger item that you sell. Clerks sell the one item. True professionals capture the add-on sales that are available to them.

The important thing here is, look around your store. (Or, if you're in outside sales, think about what resources you have available to bundle or package with your core sales items.) In every situation, have an idea of what you might add into the sale. Practice it (or them) so you can do it smoothly, and the consumer will be apt to think that you came up with each idea with only them in mind. I assure you it will be easier to do than you might believe.

As you look around for items to include in a bundle sale, you may very well find that there are many things you can add to the major items you sell. The same add-on sales items might be added to many different major items. It's imperative that you have approximate numbers in your head as a guide to how much a principle item may cost a consumer and how financing a secondary, bundle item would add to the monthly payments. You can double-check the payment book when you're close to the sale; but getting the book out too early can sometimes make your consumer or client uneasy.

You should be prepared to talk in generalities about how a monthly payment might be affected by an add-on sale. You'll find that this isn't very difficult once you take a few minutes to look at a payment guide and familiarize yourself with the numbers. You can find free payment guides online, and of course there are books available. Your employer may provide one. If not, then please do it yourself.

Sales Whisperer™ Tip #13

Don't confine yourself to thinking that the rationalization technique we just discussed is applicable only to financed items. You can use the same process to close bundled sales even when consumers pay cash. You can still talk about the average life of the major and bundled items you're selling. Relate that combined cost to the consumer as an up-charge of X amount more per month, week, or day, and it will have the same positive effect on them.

Incremental sales provide a number of positive results. For example, you will:

- increase your gross sales.
- improve the mix of business you and your store enjoy in the marketplace, which allows you and your employer to aggressively improve the financial health of your operation.
- ensure that your business or store becomes more of a one-stop-shop for consumers considering future purchases.
- convince the consumer that you can provide the RIGHT items along with the RIGHT peripherals at the RIGHT price.

- enhance the consumer's buying experience.

- improve consumer loyalty.

You'll be more financially successful whether you work in a store, are part of an outside sales force, or are an independent entrepreneur. Using human psychology and the power of rationalization will help you achieve your rightful place as a leader in your industry.

Do you know how to tell the difference between the true professionals, weak salespeople, and most clerks (who are paid a straight salary with no incentive to sell more)? Check the parking lot. The true professionals are much more likely to arrive in newer and more expensive cars. And you know what? They EARNED that privilege, and I say, "Good for them!"

Chapter 10

After-Sale Selling

Your selling job isn't over just because money has changed hands. If your intent is to exceed your consumer's expectations and continue your control (or leadership) that you worked so hard to attain, following up after the sale is imperative. Remember, when I say control I'm referring to maintaining their image of you as the ONLY person they would choose to guide them through any other major purchase of items you sell. This also reinforces in their minds that you're someone who they can confidently recommend to a friend or relative, knowing that you won't let them down. Referrals, and the ability to get a lot of them, ensure that the successful sales professional stands out among contemporaries and competitors.

When consumers buy something from you, particularly when they do so because of the confidence you engendered by utilizing the Sales Whisperer™ program, they not only buy your product, concept, or idea, they buy into YOU. Capitalize on this. After all, using this method, you uncovered the true bottom-line benefits germane to their situation, and you helped them resolve that situation.

You did not SELL them anything. You orchestrated the proper environment to allow them to make an informed purchase decision. You helped them rationalize—to themselves, their families, and their friends—why they made a particular purchase decision and why it was a prudent decision. How many salespeople have you run into who really do that well without using the tenets of the Sales Whisperer™ psychology that you're currently learning? I'm guessing the answer is very few.

Yes I Care

So here is what you do after the money has changed hands: you implement what I call the Yes I Care program. Some salespeople take the time to send a thank you note to their consumers, and that's a step in the right direction. Most of the notes, however, look pretty vanilla—and like a form letter. I suggest that you mark your planner to remind yourself to call consumers the day after the scheduled delivery or installation. Thank them again for their purchase. Let them know that this is standard operating procedure for you, that you call ALL of your consumers the day after delivery. If you're selling real estate, call the day after they move in.

If they didn't purchase a service policy when they bought from you, this is not the time to sell one. NEVER try to sell them a service policy during this call. That is not the purpose of the follow-up call. Refraining from attempting any sort of additional sale makes the consumer believe that your call is sincere, as opposed to the normal consumer follow-up.

Below are some of the things you SHOULD say.

"I just wanted to make sure the delivery and installation went well for you." You might be hesitant to call, believing that a statement like this invites trouble. My contention (and my experience backs this up) is that they probably would have called you anyway if they had a problem. Why not be proactive? Make their problem go away; you would have to anyway. The difference is that they'll forever remember that you were sincere and professional enough to follow up on your sale. Exactly what do you think they'll tell their neighbors? Most of the time it will be something like, "When you're ready to buy that new bed, go to ABC Furniture and MAKE SURE YOU TALK TO JOE! He's the best." They'll tell their neighbors how they were treated and how you followed up on the sale.

You can also say, **"I'll bet that new coffee table looks even better in your living room than you anticipated."** Or, **"I'm sure that you're already enjoying the benefits of that new (whatever it is)!"** Whatever you say, make it positive. When you're satisfied that everything is as it should be, thank them again for their purchase and trust in you. Remind them that you would appreciate any referrals they send to you, and promise that you'll treat them right.

I learned this concept from an older woman I worked with early in my career, who saw that I could close but didn't have many repeat consumers. She knew that my sales were high overall, and that I had an exceptional track record of selling service policies that paid a higher commission rate than most of the products I sold. She thought, however, that I was a little too ruthless, and offered to help me. I'm not the smartest guy in the world, but I did a very wise thing when I swallowed my ego and actually listened. She was mightily successful and much respected, and on an almost daily basis, she shared her philosophy and honest and forthright approach to sales. Unknown to me, the foundation of the Sales Whisperer™ technique had been laid. I combined her philosophy with my research on human psychology to start closing more sales.

Yes I Care means so much to the consumer, more than even a hand-written thank you note. That note ends up in the trashcan. My brief phone call is burned into the consumer's memory as no note ever could be. Implement Yes I Care, and I assure you, you'll immediately start enjoying a positive return on a small investment of your time.

At this point, it's important to address the most successful way to handle angry clients, whether it happens during a Yes I Care phone call or not. There are a few simple rules that act like the cushioning technique we discussed in Chapter 7: "Handling Consumer Objections." In my experience, you must follow these rules to maximize success in handling upset clients or consumers.

Acknowledge the consumer's anger immediately

In order for you to come out the hero or heroine again, somebody has to be the calming force in this encounter. That's your job. You must not allow this to escalate into a confrontation. If you don't allow consumers to vent, their anger will intensify, they'll never be happy, and will not only fail to recommend you; they may inform their friends to avoid you and the company you represent. Instead, do something that is very difficult for an extrovert like you to do during a trying time: Listen intently and say only the few words required to show empathy for their concerns.

Show your concern

Use the cushioning techniques you learned earlier. This lets them know that you take their anger seriously, but don't do it so frequently that you interrupt their perfectly good vent.

Don't rush the conversation

Be patient and they'll eventually calm down, particularly if you don't fuel their anger by trying to argue with them or fix the problem too quickly. Many times, after they calm down they realize that you're not arguing with them. They might even acknowledge that you may not personally be the cause of their problem, and that your helpful personality is consistent with what they experienced when they bought from you in the first place. Many times, they'll feel that they were too hard on you, and feel a little guilty for taking it out on you simply because you're the only company representative they know. When this happens, you have the perfect environment for compromise.

Ask fact-finding questions

Ask fact-finding or discovery questions to identify the error and what difficulty it has caused. When you're sure of what happened, consider what you have the authority to offer without seeking management approval—assuming that you're not the owner. Once you have a possible "fix" in mind, say, "I'm terribly sorry and shocked that this happened to you. This isn't normal, I assure you. What do you think a reasonable resolution would be?" You are then aware of what they specifically desire and, because you handled this in the proper way, more times than you would think they'll ask for something less than what you're authorized to offer. If that's the case, give the discount for damaged goods, offer to replace the product, give a discount for a future purchase because your delivery people were rude, or anything you need to do to satisfy them on the spot.

If, on the other hand, you don't have the authority to make amends for the problem, tell your consumers that you'll represent them to the manufacturer of the product or to your boss, and that you'll get back to them in a timely manner. Then be sure to get back to them as quickly as you promised. Once you find out what you can offer, do NOT, if at all possible, let your boss call them on your behalf. YOU sold this consumer. YOU enjoy the commission on the sale. They contacted YOU about the problem, and YOU want to be the person who communicates the resolution of the problem. In this way, YOU solved the problem and they'll turn to YOU in the future when they need something that you sell.

I promise you: there will be situations where you or someone else makes a mistake, and this is the best (and time-tested) way to turn lemons into lemonade. In the end, you may earn even more respect from the consumer than you had when you sold them the product. They may very well become fiercely loyal to you because of how you handled this situation. You demonstrated, clearly, what they suspected and hoped for when they purchased a product from you. They are now confident that when they need to purchase something in the future you'll "walk the talk" that you demonstrated when they first spent their hard-earned money with you. You'll be "the real deal" to them—and that's a precious commodity for people who have to invest in something that's beyond the range of their expertise.

When this happens, you now have created EXACTLY what every sales professional wants: You can add them to your list of consumers for life! Even if you change companies, if you do a good job of keeping your consumer list and contact numbers up to date, and contact them with the new location in which you'll be hanging your hat, they WILL FOLLOW. And THAT is a very good position in which to be.

Chapter 11

Dealing with Executives

This chapter is devoted to the care and feeding of executives. Some salespeople are intimidated when dealing with executives. The more powerful the executive, the higher the fear factor is for the uninformed. Once you understand the characteristics of executives, the easier it is to sell a product, service, concept, or idea. We all have worked for executives, and told jokes about how decisive and cold these folks can be. We have a mental picture of how difficult it would be to deal with them on a one-on-one basis. Perception isn't always reality, but there are some common traits of top executives you need to familiarize yourself with to help ensure success or raise your odds of having a successful meeting with them.

Before we get into that, I'd like to share four short jokes that are frequently passed around between employees. They demonstrate (and help form) our opinions of how executives, particularly top executives, think. They can be filed under Memos That Would Be Communicated By Executives Within The Company—If They Felt They Could Get Away With Them.

1. "We will no longer accept a doctor's excuse as proof of sickness. If you're able to go to the doctor to get an excuse, you're able to come to work!"

2. "Entirely too much time is being spent in the restrooms. There is now a strict three-minute time limit in the stalls. At the end of three minutes, an alarm will sound, the toilet paper roll will retract, the stall door will open, and a picture will be taken. After your second offense, you will be labeled a chronic offender, and your picture will be posted on the company's intranet with 100% distribution. Anyone caught smiling in the picture will be sanctioned under the company's mental health policy."

3. "We are here to provide a positive employment experience. Therefore, all questions, comments, concerns, complaints, frustrations, irritations, aggravations, insinuations, allegations, contemplation, consternation, and input should be directed…elsewhere."

4. "Firing will continue around here until morale improves."

These jokes foster fear in salespeople, and employees for that matter, and makes them approach (not greet) executives with great trepidation. If you understand what is important to executives, you can handle them with relative ease. Let's examine the important points to consider when selling to the "executive type."

Be prepared

DO YOUR HOMEWORK ON THE COMPANY BEFORE THE MEETING. This seems so obvious, even trite, but many more people than you might think fail to do it.

- If it's a public company, get a shareholder's report and study the mission statement and financials.
- Get a 10K report and review it.
- Get a Dunn & Bradstreet report.
- Search the Internet for information.
- Visit the company's website.
- Talk to employees of the company.
- Visit the facility.

Joe Panzica

It's imperative that you demonstrate, throughout the conversation, that you've done your homework on where the company is now—and where they want to be. This is an important objective for an executive. Be prepared to tailor your benefit stories toward supporting the achievement of this objective. Make it look like each benefit will make their job easier and expedite the attainment of that objective. Present a benefit for each objective you discovered during your research.

Respect the executive's time

The average executive typically has more than a weeks' worth of business on his or her desk at any one time. Be sensitive to the executive's time constraints. Make sure you're organized. Practice your presentation, and time it. Add 10% more time for unanticipated questions. When making the appointment, tell the executive how much time the meeting will take, and be prepared to live with the time frame you promised. I can say with great confidence and a lot of experience, that is one of the things on which you'll be graded.

Be direct

Executives are generally direct themselves and will appreciate your directness because it shows that you're not only time sensitive, but also a very bottom-line kind of person. In other words, you're just like them. They like doing business with people who are like them. They don't have time for small talk or peripheral conversations.

Speak the executive's language

Talk in terms of Return on Investment (ROI), Return on Equity (ROE), Return on Assets (ROA), and Earnings Before Interest, Taxes, Depreciation and Amortization (EBITDA). Specify how your product or idea will augment their efforts to improve their company's results. For the most part, this is all that matters to them. Profitability is the mainstay of their job description. Every feature you offer must deliver a benefit that will enhance profitability, whether it's time savings to increase productivity, human resource reduction through automation, lower physical distribution costs (logistics), decreased order and billing costs, or any other thing you can think of. Their absolute goal is to lower the SG&A (sales & general administration) costs.

Even if you're not selling executives anything for their business, their demeanor will, most often, remain the same. Whether you're selling an item at retail or selling them a house, it's still a business transaction, and their natural tendency will be to revert to the executive or CEO mindset. After all, you're talking about relieving them of personal finances. They're used to being good stewards of their company's resources, and they'll naturally use some of the same arguments and questions when governing their own resources.

Whether you're selling them something of a personal nature or something work-related, stay with the "Big Picture" when you talk to them. They're used to managing from a 10,000-foot level and don't want—or have the time—to get caught up in details. They have subordinates who handle the details for them. Sometimes they're even embarrassed that they no longer know how things happen in the company the way they might have earlier in their careers. They will not allow themselves to show ignorance by talking details.

Executives simply don't know or care HOW things are done, as long as they're done within budget requirements. They just tell their employees to get something done in a certain period and let them worry about the procedure. All executives want to do is make a decision, give an order to make it happen—and let their subordinates deliver the goods in a legal and ethical manner. Make sure you talk only on a macro level with them.

Remember: ONLY with executives should you state the feature, skip the function, and go right to the benefit.

Before meeting with an executive, get input from the people in the company regarding the easiest way for them to implement your product or service. If you can, get their opinion on how much time and money could be realized and identified as a measurable savings if they had your product, idea, or service. When you talk to the executive you can say, "I've checked with your people. They're impressed with the product (whatever product you're selling), and are confident of an easy transition to it. They feel that, long term, it will save the company X amount of time and X amount of money." They see that you've done your homework. This is a very impressive way to stay away from the details while communicating that you have a viable product or idea. In some cases, it takes away the "Let me talk to my people" stall or argument.

If it truly is a big-ticket item, he or she probably will talk to the people on the firing line whose opinions he or she trusts. If you talked to the same people in advance, they can be trusted to support your presentation because you have already satisfied their questions and concerns.

Men are different

Because both men and women have risen to executive positions, you have to deal with them just as you would in retail. Remember that they're still human beings. You'll recall that I said earlier that, for the most part, men and women think and process information differently. Please don't forget this; it's vital in a commercial selling situation as well as in the executive's personal life. But there are other things to remember when it comes to men. They won't apply to all men, but they certainly apply to most men, so take heed.

Men are more impulsive. They are more likely to shoot from the hip, verbally and through their actions. They're VERY decisive, whether they're right or wrong. Most male executives tend to say something like, "Just do it. If it works, great. We don't waste time in implementation. If it's wrong we'll change on the fly."

Now, don't let me confuse the issue here. I know that there are certain things that no executive would do quickly, because of the financial implications; however, you need to remain cognizant of how men think. I have seen many decisions made just like the example above. The point I'm trying to make here is simply to remember what men have a tendency to do, and then play the odds.

Men are not comfortable asking questions that would imply that they're confused or unsure. That's one reason most men never seem to ask directions, and would prefer to drive around trying to find the correct route to their destination. (Sound familiar?) This validates why you should talk to those who will actually introduce and use the product you're selling BEFORE you talk to the executive. Then, when you share the employees' approval of your product with the executive, he or she will have some assurance that those who will do the work are already sold on the idea.

Women are different

Women executives have virtually the same personality traits as male executives, with a few notable differences. Women, even executives, tend to want assurance from others who own or have used the product or service. Be prepared to offer testimonials (written, if possible) from your current consumers on the productivity and quality of what you're offering. Female executives tend to ask for (or do) more research rather than deciding on "gut feel." Let me remind you that this does not apply to all women; but again, you're playing the odds.

Actually, you should expect all executives to shoot from the hip. It's simply in the executive nature. It's one of the behavioral traits that got them where they are professionally. You need to expect and appreciate this and keep your cool when it happens. Anticipate the questions and concerns they may have, imagine what sharp comments you can expect, and practice your calm response.

Don't be put off by the directness. You need a thick skin

to prevail in sales. Remember, "It's not personal. It's just business." A frightening statement if you're looking down the barrel of a gun, but that's rarely the case in sales. Executives who are direct are just being themselves and trying to get quickly to the bottom line. It's what they do. It's who they are. Accept it, don't be surprised by it, and prepare yourself to deal with it. Based on my personal experience (and I've had a lot of it) and the success of people I have counseled, I'm confident that if you remember what is in this chapter, you'll be able to deal with executives successfully.

People often say, "I know that great service can help me keep an executive as a client, but how can I get the executive's interest in the first place?" That's a challenge for sure, but there are some simple rules you can follow that will raise your odds of being successful on a "cold call" with executives, whether it's on the phone or in writing.

Executives want to touch each piece of paper only once. They read it, throw it away, or act on it. They simply cannot afford to be looking at the same thing numerous times, or to read something that takes too long to get to the bottom line. You and I would feel the same way in their position. With that in mind, make sure that you keep your initial contact with them to one page and one page only. Make sure the letter reflects YOU, particularly if this is your first contact. If you're naturally casual, then make the correspondence casual. If you're naturally formal, make the letter appropriately formal.

Open with an endorsement. For example, "Is it any wonder that executives from ABC Company, XYZ Corporation, and Walter's Widgets, Inc. utilize my services?" Follow the endorsement directly, and briefly, with the benefits you can offer to this particular executive and the company he or she represents.

Itemize your information. Use bullet points to get your information across succinctly. Be direct by staying on point. Use no details! Remember, they have subordinates who will handle the details. Instead, do what research you can in advance to assure them (in very few words) that you've done your homework and that the details can be easily worked out because of it. Remember the different ways that most men and women tend to learn and process information. List your strengths and your company's strengths. Talk in terms of ROI, ROE, ROA, and EBITDA. End with an action statement, such as, "Call me by April 15." Or, "I'll follow up with a phone call on April 15."

Sell your image—and make sure that image is as closely related to the executive's as you can make it. When you're dealing with executives, you're dealing with star power. You should be a star at what you do, so present yourself like the professional you are. Talk and act like you are on the executive's level. I recall a high-powered, talented, wholesale salesperson that used to work for me who once asked, "How much power do my clients think I have with our company?" My response? "Exactly as much power as you lead them to believe you have." If you act like an underling when talking to an executive, expect to be treated like one.

And finally, remember that executives are bottom-line people with no time for superfluous information. They're pragmatic and mathematical. The two questions they'll always ask themselves are:

"Does this meet my needs?" And, "Will this solve my problem?"

It's your job to make sure that the answer to both is yes.

Chapter 12

Some Proven Ways to Suspect Lies

In any form of sales, it's important to be able to detect whether or not your client, consumer, or buyer is fabricating the truth in order to put you under pressure or to gain a negotiation advantage. If someone is lying to you, you are not in control of the selling situation.

But consumers never lie, do they? Of course they do. Do you? Have you ever told a "white lie" in order to get a better deal on a car? Ever quoted a fictitious price another dealership "gave" you, trying to get the price down on the car you want? Did you ever tell the salesperson that you got the other dealer to throw in options at no charge when it really didn't happen? I'm quite sure we have all tried at some time to gain an unfair advantage when negotiating price, terms, or conditions for something we wanted—and slept very well that night—because we convinced ourselves that it was all part of the negotiation game. We rationalized that the salesperson probably got us on something and we needed to offset that—if not gain more than we lost—through any means possible, even lying.

Why should your consumers or buyers be any different?

So how can you tell when or if someone is lying? The rice test, used in ancient China, is curiously effective and costs virtually nothing. The subject puts a handful of uncooked rice in his mouth. The premise is that guilt tends to dry saliva, making the rice stick to the tongue and the roof of the mouth. After a short time, the subject spits out the rice and opens his mouth. If there is an excess of rice on the roof of the mouth or the tongue, the assumption is that he's lying. This method, while cost-effective, isn't very practical in a sales situation. Can you imagine saying to a consumer (or vice versa), "Would you put this rice in your mouth, please?"

The polygraph, often referred to as a lie detector test, works on the same principle as the rice test, by measuring physiological arousal and brain activity associated with emotional stress, such as increased heart rate, pulse, and respiration, and conductivity of the skin. Introduced in 1913, the polygraph was a step in the right direction toward sure-fire lie detection, but it's neither infallible nor admissible in most courts. It can and does indicate that a person MAY be lying, but cannot definitively interpret the results.

For example, if a robbery suspect takes a polygraph test, she might have a physiological reaction to the question, "Did you rob this bank?" Even though she may not have robbed the bank, the word bank might cause a measurable reaction because she bounced a check the week before. This unpleasant memory might trigger a reaction, leading to what is known as a false positive. (Wade and Tavris 2004, 404-406)

I guess for our purpose that's all well and good; how many of the people you negotiate with would let you hook them up to a polygraph? (It would be fun though, wouldn't it?) Dr. Paul Ekman, Professor Emeritus at California University, and Dr. Maureen O'Sullivan, from San Francisco University (wasn't there a movie star by that name?), are developing programs to train federal agents to recognize deceit. It seems that there are a small number of people who are extraordinarily good at detecting lies—with up to 90% accuracy. (Adelson 2004) Perhaps someday, thanks to Drs. Ekman and O'Sullivan, we'll all be highly trained in lie detection, but that's probably a long way off.

So how DO you know when a consumer is lying? There are no sure-fire ways to tell, but there are signs that can indicate deceit—or at least raise a red flag during your conversation or negotiation.

Eye Contact

The consensus is that if someone avoids eye contact, there's a good chance that he or she is lying, but you cannot be sure. Experienced poker players don't put much confidence in what they call "eye tells." The other players could be bluffing, or it might be natural for them not to look people in the eye due to shyness or low self-esteem. It's also normal for some people to look away while formulating an answer; they want to stare at something, an inanimate object, for example, while they think. If a person looks away while GIVING an answer to a relatively simple question, however, you should at least wonder why. On the other hand, people telling a "white lie" may actually INCREASE their eye contact to convince you that they're being truthful. If you notice an increase in focus and intensity of eye contact, odds are that they're trying too hard to convince you, and the reason for that could be a lie in progress.

Blinking

The average person blinks 12 to 20 times a minute. When people lie, they tend to blink much more—some more than 45 times per minute. If someone blinks more in response to some questions than to others, he or she may be lying about those answers.

Vocal Inflection

Be aware of changes in pitch or rate of speech. An increased use of non-words, such as "Um" and "Ah," compared to what you previously observed, may indicate lying.

Misleading Behavior in Those Written Words

Dr. James Pennebaker, professor of psychology at the University of Texas at Austin, developed a software program known as Linguistic Inquiry and Word Count, or LIWC, which is 67% effective in detecting written lies compared to 52% accuracy for humans reading the same material. As with the polygraph and the rice test, you're unlikely to be able to apply the software to your consumer's written communication. Pennebaker says, however, that those who lie in writing tend to use fewer first-person pronouns (I, me, my, mine) in order to "distance themselves from their stories and avoid taking responsibility for their behavior." (Adelson 2004).

For example, someone might say, "THE paperwork was sent yesterday," rather than the direct and more personal "I sent it yesterday." If you notice a lack of first-person pronouns in a consumer's written communications with you, pay attention. The consumer may be lying.

Body Language

There is no such person as Pinocchio and unfortunately, nobody's nose is going to grow rapidly right in front of you when they lie. Consider, instead, the total person. Is there a mismatch between what's going on in one part of the body and the others? If so, watch and listen to them with more intensity for two reasons: first, you want to focus on what they're doing so you can determine whether they might be lying or not; and second, you want them to know you're concentrating on their behavior so you can see how they react when they realize that you're watching them closely. Watch what they do when you suspect they may be lying.

If they use gestures more than normal, be very mindful that something could be amiss. Concentrate on small changes in hand movements and the number of gestures, and note whether they are consistent with what's coming out of their mouths. Some people talk with their hands quite a bit, and it's normal for them. This is why you have to become a strong observer.

Hand movements are fairly telling, so watch for those. If someone holds his hands out so that you can see his palms, it generally means that he is open to you—to the point of being vulnerable—because he trusts you. As you know, a fist can mean anger when someone is making a point. When she holds her hand higher than normal while gesturing, it means that she feels what she is saying is a stronger argument than what you're saying. (It's kind of like when we were kids and you said, "My Dad can beat up your Dad.") When people do this, normally they're expressing their sense of superiority over what you're offering or saying.

Sitting with hands folded doesn't mean that he is praying for mercy! It could very well mean (and does, in many cases) that he is closed to your idea and needs further convincing. Pointing with one finger means that this point is important to her. Pointing with two fingers emboldens the effort in her mind. If someone holds a pencil or pen in one hand the whole time and gestures with it, he or she generally feels that they're the conductor in this and any other situation. If they hold it with the fingertips of both hands, they're closing you off a little, putting a little barrier between you and them. If they click a pen in and out constantly, they're impatient. If they click it constantly only when they're making a point, they want to emphasize the importance of that point.

If a quiet person talks a lot, or a person who usually talks gets quiet, probe a little deeper. Odds are they're not being totally truthful with you. Some people who don't talk much may talk more when they're nervous; and others who are normally extroverts tend to clam up a little when nervous. Either way, the person may not be lying, but it's a definite red flag. Measure this reaction against their normal behavior.

Any kind of change in body posture should be suspicious to you. Some people slump more when they're lying, others tend to stand or sit straighter when they're lying. The determining factor is whether they do anything different from the norm (for them). If so, question the validity or motive of what they say.

It's Not the Smile It's the TYPE of Smile

You can easily tell sincere smiles from insincere smiles (those executed to cover anger, sadness, or disgust). True smiles involve not just the lips but also the muscles around the eyes. When someone is happy or amused you'll see a very relaxed, animated smile that truly affects the eyes. Some people squint quite a bit when they smile. Others intensify what is already a droopy eye. In some, you can actually see their eyes dancing with glee. Liars will try to mask their smiles.

Micro-expressions

As part of his research, Dr. Ekman has identified what he calls "micro-expressions," ultra-brief facial expressions that reveal what people are truly feeling or thinking. (Adelson 2004) You have to watch for these very closely because they are what they are called, tiny-expressions; but they're worth looking for when you suspect someone is lying. They happen quickly because the liar is trying hard not to disclose that he or she is in fact lying. People cannot stop micro-expressions; they're an automatic response by the body and while they're brief timewise, they can sometimes be very animated. If, in answer to a serious question, you see a smile start, even from one side of the mouth only, but it's quickly suppressed, watch for other signs of lying.

Other Things to Observe

- Fully or partially covering the mouth when answering a question.

- Turning away, even slightly, during some of their answers.

- Contradicting themselves. If you have reason to suspect a lie, try asking your question in a couple of different ways and see if you get the same answer.

As you can see, detecting lies isn't a perfect science. The polygraph is an indicator with some scientific merit, but it's certainly not practical in a business environment. Nevertheless, psychologists have given us some tools that will make you more effective in your scrutiny of liars or suspected liars.

Chapter 13

Effective Presentation Skills

Whether talking to one consumer or to a group of people in a formal setting, use proper presentation skills. Practice your presentation skills so that the words roll off your tongue in a very natural and seemingly unrehearsed way.

In 1995, I attended a seminar at Harvard University. The participants were upper management and company presidents from retail and wholesale. We were divided into three ten-person teams, given case studies of three companies to review, and instructed to put together specific ideas to improve the gross revenue and maintained margin of profit for each company. Each team presented its recommendations to the other two teams, the dean of the MBA program, and MBA students, who took copious notes.

While I believed deeply in all of the strategies presented, I stressed that, based on what I noticed when visiting stores in different cities, sales skills are sorely needed at the store level as well. Sorely needed, and often overlooked. What follows is the information I shared at Harvard. I hope you'll study and use it in your morning preparation each day.

I talked briefly about some of these things in the selling segment; but repeating them will provide a redundancy of learning. I teach these things in my Professional Formal Presentation Skills seminar. They'll guide you in making compelling presentations, within and without your company, and increase your sales skills overall.

Remember, whether you're doing a formal meeting or meeting a consumer for the first time, you need to establish your personal objectives for that day, week, or month. Be very clear about what you want to accomplish and about your strategy for attaining that objective, so that you can measure your results. Remember, too, that people use their senses to process information. Learn how to size people up based on the information presented in Chapter 2.

Make sure your delivery techniques make sense. Keep pocket change and jewelry quiet. In fact, try not to have change in your pocket at any time. Don't wear an excessive amount of jewelry, and never wear jewelry that makes noise every time you move. You want the consumer or audience to focus on YOU rather than distractions. Some people in the audience may not even want to be there and have attended only because the boss told them to. Most consumers are only seeking your help because they have a problem that they hope you can help them economically resolve. Neither the audience nor the consumer needs any excuse to lose focus and ignore what you're saying.

Use appropriate words. Obviously, you prove nothing by using profanity, but this also reflects back to what we talked about before: Professionals use the correct manufacturer or industry's terminology. If I'm spending my hard-earned money or any of my hard-pressed time, I want to do it with a professional and nothing less, and I'm sure you're the same way.

Speak clearly. You may be thinking that I'm talking about not using slang or slurring your words, and I am, but I mean more than that. I mean speak clearly and without mistake. Get your point across to your audience, client, or consumer.

Here's an example I use in my seminars: A farmer has 26 sheep. One dies. How many does he have left? Now, most people say, "25." The first time I heard this, I tried to be coy, and said, "The farmer would still have 26 sheep. But one would just be dead!" This generates a laugh, which is my intention, but then I say that I didn't say that the farmer had

26 sheep—I said that the farmer had 20 sick sheep and one of them died. Had I articulated correctly, the audience would have understood that I said not 26 but 20 SICK sheep, and that the correct answer was that the farmer had 19 sheep left. Say this out loud, and you'll see how important it is to articulate and to think about what you're saying.

Maintain an interesting rate of speech. It's okay to raise and lower your voice to make a point. Just make sure that you don't stay at the same volume all the way through the presentation (during the Feature-Function-Benefit section, for example). Practice the use of strategic pauses before making meaningful points. I provided an example of strategic pauses in Chapter 2, when I talked about how men and women learn. Pauses and silence can be the most effective way to foster positive anticipation for your answer or the benefit you're explaining. I've said before that salespeople are, by nature, extroverts and that we tend to think out loud. But it's far more effective to use strategic pauses than it is to listen to yourself ramble. Use pauses to make a major point.

Do NOT use non-words like "um," "ah," or "okay?" Don't use phrases like "you know," or "you see." When you do this, you tell the consumer that you're unsure of what you're saying, and that dilutes their confidence in you. If you must use non-words as part of your thought process, say them to yourself and pause only as long as it takes you to say the non-word (to YOURSELF!) While you do that, look knowingly at whoever asked the question. When we use non-words, we're trying to buy ourselves a second to formulate an answer. You can still do this, but rather than stammering a non-word and letting the consumer think that they've stumped you, pause strategically and consumers instead feel that they've asked an intelligent question. They also see that you kept your cool and acted like a professional while you formulated your answer.

Don't pace! Pacing sends the message that you're nervous. It's easy to pace during a formal presentation, but it happens to some salespeople during the sales presentation, as well. They pace, or constantly shift their weight from one leg to the other, or keep walking back and forth between the consumer and the product. If the consumer or audience thinks that you're nervous, what do you suppose they think is the reason? If you pace, they'll believe that you're nervous because you're inexperienced or that you're not sure of your response's accuracy. They might feel that you'll guess at an answer just to look better in front of them. Worse, they could and in some cases do, suspect that the next words out of your mouth will be an absolute fabrication. You lose control at that point and those listening tune you out—which is the worst thing that can happen in any kind of a selling situation.

So what can you do to release the tension or nervousness that might manifest itself because of a consumer objection or a tough and unexpected question? You can partial pace for starters. If you're making a formal presentation, you can take a few steps to the left and then WHILE STANDING STILL talk to the left side of the audience. Move a few steps to your right and STAND STILL while you direct the rest of your answer to the right side of the room. Try not to do this in a one-on-one selling situation.

Something that you can do in a one-on-one selling situation, which is also very effective in a formal presentation, is to simply pause (strategically, of course) and curl your toes toward the floor. This will burn energy and the consumer or group will never see you doing this with your toes—unless you're barefoot and standing on the beach! You only need to press your toes to the floor for two seconds and then release. Repeat the procedure if you must, but never for longer than a couple of seconds at a time.

Yet another technique is to take a deep breath. Now, a normal deep breath will send the wrong message: that you're indeed flustered by the question or objection. There are two slam-dunk ways to take a deep breath without betraying any nervousness or surrendering control to the questioner. First, fake a yawn! SMILE and say, "Please excuse me. I was up late last night, helping my son with algebra. I'm sure you've done the same at one time or another with your own kids. It's (while smiling again) certainly not a reflection on your good question." You can also camouflage a deep breath meant to relieve tension by taking a deep breath and saying, "Well, that's an interesting question that I have been asked before." You've bought a few seconds to collect your thoughts and it conditions your audience to believe that you'll provide an intelligent answer based on your experience.

Don't lock your knees. People often do this to relieve tension and I must admit it does work very well—until they pass out because they've blocked blood flow too long! You could do this for a few seconds and then unlock your knees, but it tends to create enough movement to suggest to some consumers that you're panicking.

Use good eye contact, as discussed earlier. Don't let your eyes dart around while you search for something to say. You can look away BRIEFLY while formulating an answer with little or no repercussions, but when you give the answer, ALWAYS look the audience or the consumer straight in the eye. One way to ensure this is to use what I call the Point-Read-Deliver method. Point to the answer (if it can be pointed to) on the presentation screen or to a specific feature on a product or contract, read it, then TURN AND FACE the person who asked the question and give him or her the answer.

Always try to stay at eye level or above your audience or consumer. In a formal presentation this is easy; the audience is generally sitting down. With consumers, have them lean down and look at the fabric of a piece of furniture or sit in a car so that in either case they have to look up at you when you answer.

DON'T fold your hands in front of you when standing for any extended period. We don't want any fig leaves here! It's a distracting mannerism. Don't do it. Instead, keep your hands at your side when you talk, or gesture animatedly with them. You can release excess energy by gesturing when you speak. (This describes my style quite a bit.) Using body energy from the waist up is great for holding attention while burning up excess energy or nervousness.

Don't keep looking at your watch. So what if you might be late to leave for lunch? You're going to make a sale! If you must look at your watch, act as if you're scratching your arm or picking a piece of lint off your sleeve, and steal a glance at the time. You can also turn your head and fake a cough, briefly covering your mouth with the hand that's attached to the arm that's home for your watch! Don't do this often, though.

Use humor if you can. An audience or consumer's retention rate increases when you use humor. And of course, your humor must be appropriate. Here are some humor Dos and Don'ts.

- Do use humor, but be sensitive to the person or persons to whom you're talking.

- Do use personal stories, if applicable, to humanize yourself.

- Do use current events.

- ALWAYS turn the humor toward yourself.

- Don't be sarcastic.

- Don't use negative humor.

- NEVER use ethnic, gender, or suggestive humor.

Be accurate in your communication; specificity should be a hallmark of your presentation. Cover items one thought at a time, and confirm understanding. Use a logical sequence in your presentation. For example, if you're talking about health insurance, you can use Feature-Function-Benefit and say, "This is a great feature in our policy for you. Here is how it works, and here is the benefit it provides you so that you can be assured of comprehensive coverage." If you're selling a grandfather clock, start at the top and work your way down. Never open the door to talk about the pendulum more than once, for example. When you get to the pendulum, open the door and talk about it, then close the door and don't open it again—even if you think of something you missed. Constant opening and closing disrupts the consumer's concentration and you don't want that.

If you think of a big feature benefit you forgot, say to the consumer, "Now you open the door and see how solid it is." While it's open, you can say, "Also…" and then cover the forgotten feature benefit. Then close the door and move on. If you think of yet another feature benefit that would require you to open the door again, forget it unless the consumer asks a specific question. You must know your product better and practice the sequence of your presentation if you continually miss benefits and have to go back.

After you get buy-in (and always get buy-in) from the audience or consumer, you need to be able to make smooth transitions when moving to the next item.

To reach both visual and auditory learners, and to create a redundancy in learning, synchronize what the consumer or audience sees and hears whenever possible. I just cannot stress this point too much. Use examples, illustrations, and analogies when possible. Prepare them in advance and practice them so that their use becomes second nature.

Remember that you can turn any criticism or objection into a positive by the cushioning technique. You can also re-phrase the concern as a question, reinforcing it as a question in the consumer's mind. Then answer the question and confirm agreement before moving on. Curb criticism by continuing to be human with the consumer or client.

Remember to ask open-ended questions. Your questions must be clear, concise, and relevant. Concentrate on one point at a time. Don't attempt to "catch" consumers in a wrong answer. That will turn them off. Even if they are wrong, you can cushion them by saying, "A lot of people ask me that, and it's a good question. When they learned the reason for it, they changed their mind." Respond with authority, but allow for the pressure the consumers feel when you correct them. You must keep your consumers focused, you must show your concern, and you must be ready to shield their ego with your answers

You are the leader and you should always be leading. Sometimes a person will say something totally out of context to the conversation. Never say that they're wrong. Simply respond with a cushion, such as, "That's an interesting point," and then continue. You're not arguing but you're not agreeing with them either. Saying that their comment is interesting keeps them on your side.

Anticipate and prepare for likely questions. Thank the audience or consumer, congratulate them on the astuteness of their question, and then answer it fully. Verify that you've answered the question and then move on. Never imply that a question is inappropriate, and never respond with an inappropriate answer.

There is certainly much more to making a professional presentation than the few nuggets shared in this chapter, but I've pointed out the similarities between dealing with one or two consumers or clients and talking to large groups. You can clearly see that you can utilize a lot of the same skills to gain and maintain control of a group or a selling situation. Put this information in your memory bank so that you can summon it when a situation calls for it, and you'll be pleased with the results.

Chapter 14

Color Psychology

Psychologists have long known that color can affect moods and behavior. Painters and lighting designers use color to set the tone and mood of a painting or theatrical production. Those who practice alternative medicine may use color to promote healing. The colors of the walls in hospitals, waiting rooms, and even offices are often chosen to soothe, calm, and reduce stress.

You can use color to your advantage in formal presentations (handouts, flyers, and overheads), or to sell an idea, concept, or product to your consumers, buyers, or clients. Color psychology is particularly important in retail sales as it can make store signage, flyers, and even price tags more effective. Forget about your favorite color: When you're aware of the connotations of colors, they can be a very important tool in your Sales Whisperer™ toolbox.

Red: Red creates excitement. It suggests strength. It's the easiest color to see—which is why stoplights and stop signs are red.

Yellow: Sunshine, warmth, safety, and happiness come to mind when we see yellow. When combined with blue or aqua, it makes us think of being on a beach watching the tide come in. You may want to use bold type so that your message really stands out.

Blue: Blue is the color most often used to elicit a sense of trust. (Is that important in sales? You bet it is.) It reminds people of clear skies, clear sailing, and even daydreaming! Advertisers use this color to promote the concepts of reliability, coolness, and cleanness. Some consumers say that blue also suggests freshness.

Green: Trees, grass, and even baseball (because of its association with spring) come to mind when we see this color. We think of nature, positive weather conditions, and successful crops. And, since paper money is green, we even equate green with wealth.

Pink: Yes, this color often does suggest femininity. Images of softness, nurturing, and sweetness come to mind. The image of motherhood, and the trust you had in your mother can be projected by the color pink. Knowing how pure and safe that is to most people, certain situations and products cry out for pink.

Purple: Purple has always been the color of power, whether we're talking about kings or powerful religious figures. By now, we're conditioned to think of purple as expensive, royal, important, spiritual, and dignified. Use purple when you want to stand out or suggest high-end quality.

Orange: This may well be the color that is least used in online marketing. When used in pop-up ads it tends to lose its hue and doesn't deliver the desired impact. Other types of media, however, get good results when using orange to convey playfulness or even a child-like atmosphere. It's a vibrant, little-used color that exudes boldness and confidence and adds warmth to whatever you're selling. It puts people in a joyful, carefree, happy mood. If you want participants to think your seminars are fun, use orange.

Gold: Gold has always been more valuable than other precious metals, such as silver or platinum. All our lives we've heard that gold is scarce and worth a lot; and when something or someone is special we say that they are worth their weight in gold. Something printed on gold conveys that same sense of worth, so save it for important, positive messages. As with yellow, use bold type.

Silver: Think prestige. While a step below gold, consumers get a very good feeling about the color silver. Like orange, it doesn't show its true strength in a power point presentation, but there is still a place for silver when you want to create a sense of something cold, scientific, and high-tech. Silver promotes the idea of Modern with a capital M.

White: Although not technically a color, we think of and refer to white as a color, and it affects our senses just as colors do. We see white as pure, clean, mild, virginal, and even youthful, with purity being the most common connotation sought by advertisers.

Black: Like white, black is not technically a true color. Still, it suggests class, elegance, and sophistication (as in black-tie affairs). Black is mysterious and seductive.

While you must always consider age, gender, and nationality when selling, keep in mind that different cultures have different psychological reactions to the same colors. The meanings listed above apply mostly to those in Western countries. Remember, too, that there are other colors, which you can easily research. See if any of them suggest the image you want to project to consumers or buyers.

Earlier in the book, I talked about the five senses and how important they are during the last three feet of the sale. Remember that many people tend to learn or process information by what they see. Please consider using colors and their connotations to enhance your power position in the selling situation. Using the right colors on your signage or verbiage can and will add yet another weapon to your arsenal.

Start selling in living color now!

Conclusion

The sales profession is a noble one. It helps the overall economy. Think about how sensitive Wall Street is to wholesale and retail sales numbers. The stock market watches these numbers very closely, and stocks rise and fall with these reports.

Salespeople are the catalyst for keeping factories running at near capacity, keeping people employed, keeping the ships at sea full of merchandise, and creating new jobs. The sales profession provides the revenue to underwrite research and engineering for newer, improved, and more sophisticated products designed to improve the lives of many people. It is indeed a profession of which to be proud, and you should feel good about the fact that you chose it as your vocation.

The fact that you've read this book tells me that you care about performing the job with honesty and integrity—and with a desire to close more sales. My experience tells me that you'll meet your objectives if you apply the psychology and practice the techniques. I strongly believe that you will increase your income, that you will bring attention to yourself for promotion opportunities, and that you will serve your consumers in a way that will make their lives a little easier.

If you do that, I will be proud to number you among the true, professional Sales Whisperers™!

Good luck and may God bless you.

Appendix

Sales Whisperer™ Tips

Sales Whisperer™ Tip #1

It is far better—and easier—to unveil something new and different at the Feature-Function-Benefit part of the presentation than in response to an objection later.

Sales Whisperer™ Tip #2

Sell the benefits. If you imagine "What's in it for me?" stamped on the forehead of every one of your clients, consumers, or buyers, you will always remember to sell the benefits.

Sales Whisperer™ Tip #3

Presentation without demonstration is just conversation.

Sales Whisperer™ Tip #4

Get the consumer physically involved when you demonstrate features in order to sell the benefit.

Sales Whisperer™ Tip #5

Don't believe in "Be-backs." When consumers leave, most of the time they don't come back.

Sales Whisperer™ Tip #6

Always put the blame on yourself when handling consumer objections.

Sales Whisperer™ Tip #7

Always give your consumers the "Yeah, buts" for which they're looking.

Sales Whisperer™ Tip #8

Consumers need you to orchestrate a rationalization moment in order to free them to make a purchase decision. Always use a chart when consumers must make a large financial decision and they clearly need to weigh the pros and cons.

Sales Whisperer™ Tip #9

Allow consumers to close the sale themselves.

Sales Whisperer™ Tip #10

When using a direct close, once you make the statement or ask the question, shut up!

Sales Whisperer™ Tip #11

Sell service policies! You get extra commission, the consumer is protected, and your company enhances its gross margin dollar earnings.

Sales Whisperer™ Tip #12

If you can imagine it, you can sell it by bundling or packaging it with any larger item that you sell.

Sales Whisperer™ Tip #13

You can close bundled sales even when consumers pay cash. Relate the combined cost to the consumer as an up-charge of X amount more per month, week, or day.

Sales Whisperer™ Tip #14

ALWAYS be truthful and forthright. Never guess at anything. If you don't know the answer, find it. Use the Sales Whisperer™ psychology to help your clients or consumers and they will line your pockets with commission and/or profits and you will feel good about yourself and your accomplishments.

Bibliography

Adelson, Rachel. "Detecting Deception." *Monitor on Psychology* 35. 7 (2004), http://www.apa.org/monitor/julaug04/detecting.html. (accessed June 3, 2007).

Wade, Carole, and Carol Tavris. *Psychology*. 7 ed. Upper Saddle River, NJ: Prentice Hall, 2003.

Acknowledgments

Nobody writes and researches a book without it being a sacrifice on those who have helped him or her. This book is no exception. My wife Mary put up with my coast-to-coast travels and with my leaving the country for meetings over the years. I also was gone on weekends when required. She spent many nights trying to sleep while I burned the midnight oil, trying to steal time to put together the words that have been flying around in my mind for many years. My daughters Stacy and Jennifer spent a few years with ol' Dad not being around for extended periods of time. In spite of which they have become great wives and mothers while growing their professional careers. I am proud of them and the support they have given me.

My sister Linda lent her technical expertise while I was using computer programs with which I was not well versed. Tom Carson gave me the final push to actually take the time to pull together my thoughts and write a book based on what I've been preaching for years. He also did the first reading of the manuscript and gave some very helpful suggestions. Barbara Simpson offered her skills in editing and rewrote my thoughts when warranted.

Finally, I would like to thank the students in my seminars and symposiums who have taken the psychology I teach seriously, and who have better realized their potential as true selling professionals. Those people are indeed Sales Whisperers™ in my book.

To all those above, I would like to express publicly my heart-felt appreciation of their efforts to make this book a reality.

About the Author

Joe Panzica has sold at retail, and worked at Whirlpool Corporation for 29 years, where he was Director of National Sales, National Accounts. He won back to back National Pinnacle Awards and was inducted into the Whirlpool Sales Hall of Fame.

Since his early retirement in 2001, Joe has conducted workshops and seminars on Retail Salesmanship, Coaching and Counseling Peers and Subordinates, and Add-on sales. He has trained salespeople in almost every state, as well as in Puerto Rico and Mexico.

The Sales Whisperer™ program is based on his experience, imagination, and understanding of human psychology and motivational methods. Sales professionals in real estate, retail, wholesale, and life insurance have all used the Sales Whisperer™ techniques successfully to increase sales.

Joe is currently a sales and marketing associate with 360 Associates, Inc. He continues to sell a few weeks each year to keep his personal skills sharp and to continue to research the most successful and positive ways to influence consumers.

To learn more about 360 Associates, Inc., or to schedule a Sales Whisperer™ workshop or seminar, go to www.360associates.com or visit www.the-sales-whisperer.net.

Joe lives in St. Joseph, Michigan.

Printed in the United States
87284LV00005B/55-87/A